KT-495-493

Open Heart,
Open Hands

Open Heart, Open Hands

John Glass

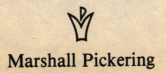

Marshall Pickering

Dedication

To my wife Marilyn for being the right inspiration.
To my friend John Lancaster for being the inspiration
to write.

Marshall Morgan and Scott
Marshall Pickering
3 Beggarwood Lane, Basingstoke, Hants RG23 7LP, UK

Copyright © 1988 John Glass
First published in 1988 by Marshall Morgan and Scott Publications Ltd
Part of the Marshall Pickering Holdings Group
A subsidiary of the Zondervan Corporation

All rights reserved. No part of this publication may be reproduced,
stored in a retrieval system, or transmitted, in any form or by any
means, electronic, mechanical, photocopying, recording or otherwise,
without the prior permission in writing, of the publisher.

ISBN: 0 551 10774 0

Text Set in Times by Brian Robinson, Buckingham
Printed in Great Britain by Cox and Wyman, Reading

Contents

Acknowledgements

Acknowledgement is due to the following for their permission to reproduce extracts from the books as indicated below.

William Barclay, *New Testament Words*, SCD Press 1964.
Os. Guiness, *The Gravedigger File*, Hodder & Stoughton.
Richard Foster, *Celebration of Discipline*, Hodder & Stoughton.
Paul E. Billheimer, *Destined for the Throne*, Christian Literature Crusade, USA.
Michael Griffiths, *Cinderella with Amnesia*, Inter-Varsity Press, USA.
Mark McCormack, *What They Don't Teach you at Harvard Business School*, Collins.
Peters, Thomas J. and Waterman, Robert H., *In Search of Excellence*, Harper and Row, Publishers, Inc.
Cory, Lloyd, *Quote Unquote*, Victor Books, Illinois.

Scripture quotes marked (NIV) are from the Holy Bible, New International Version, copyright held by Hodder & Stoughton.

1: Open Face

Jesus loves open people. Of course He loves everybody, but it is open people who, more than anyone else, appear to be the closest to His heart. Hard-faced Pharisees gaped in amazement as He talked, and even dined on occasions, with the street-people that other folk all too easily pigeon-holed as 'publicans and sinners'.

Perhaps they were openly sinful, but He was equally open with them. They knew that Jesus could reject their sin without feeling that they had been abandoned as individuals. He did not see them as souls to be saved or statistics to be gathered. He saw them as hurting people. They had far more than 'pew potential' as far as He was concerned and they knew it. They were always 'at home' with Him for He was never 'on show' with them. Open people are attracted to open people.

Pharisees, of whatever era and Judaistic or not, have always had the habit of despising both the sinner and the saint alike. Pharisees were anything but unconventional so when one by the name of Simon invited Jesus to have a meal with him it was an act which bordered on the very brink of religious dissidence – by the ground-rules of those days. However, when the ex-prostitute gate-crashed the dinner party it is certain that, could he have scheduled his filofax in retrospect, this was one engagement that would have surely been missing.

Not everyone is comfortable with the extremes of what is sometimes referred to as 'exterior worship' but what was to happen next would make the most enthusiastic Pentecostal Celebration look like a high church Latin Mass. Carrying an alabaster jar, she brings to Christ that which once had enticed clients to her, and by that act made her offering of perfume a sacrament. Tears flowed in torrents and as they dropped onto the Master's feet she wiped them away with the long tresses of her hair, then, if that was not extravagant worship enough, she kissed his feet and poured perfume up on them. One almost feels pity for the Pharisee.

Simon said nothing but his mind was in overdrive, 'If this man were a prophet he would know who was touching him – and what kind of woman she is.'[1] At that moment Simon became the spokesman for a multitide of cold souls who would sit in worship services in centuries to come and, though not always articulating their feelings, would look in silent condemnation on those who come before the Lord with tenderness and exuberance.

We are told only of the thoughts of Simon and not of his visual expression. Jesus never responds to masks: only to the heart. He revealed that truth when he observed the Pharisee and the Publican praying and again when the crowd encouraged Him to run for office and to become King. John records, 'He did not need man's testimony about man for He knew what was in man.'[2]

The word hypocrite refers to one who 'acts a part' or 'speaks from behind a mask' and when Jesus said, 'Simon I have something to tell you' – Simon lost face. Yet Jesus never unmasks anyone to harm, but to heal. It might hurt for a while but bringing us to openness is for the purpose of cleansing the wound not for turning the knife. It may produce brokenness in us but it is out of this very brokenness that Jesus brings restoration. He knows that people full of themselves can never be full of Him.

A little-known story in the Old Testament is that of Abijah the Prince and Ahijah the Prophet.[3] Jeroboam had been raised up to be King but as time went by he and his wife slowly fell into a state of spiritual backsliding. When their son Abijah became seriously ill alarm bells began to ring and they knew that only God was in a position to answer the emergency. It is a sad fact that God sometimes can only bring us to our knees by forcing us there, or put another way, God, 'Devises ways so that a banished person may not remain estranged from Him.'[4] The problem for them, as they saw it, was highly embarrassing. They were not interested in repentance and a new commitment. They were only concerned in getting their short-terms needs met and, like so many others, of using God like the spare wheel of a car – important in a crisis but then hidden away and forgotten until next time. Jeroboam thought he had discovered the solution when he suggested that his wife put on a disguise, pop off to the prophet and come back with an answer that would tide them over to the next emergency. Oh, and take him a parcel of food – possibly to tide him over till his next emergency. They were to learn that when God looks for total commitment and a repentant heart He will not be fobbed off with groceries.

Ahijah the prophet was physically blind but spiritually he had twenty-twenty vision. Before she got within a hundred yards of his house God had warned him that the Queen was coming and that, when she arrived, she would pretend to be someone else. The story, apart from its tragedy, has nearly all the ingredients of a Whitehall farce. Here was a woman in a disguise, visiting a blind man who could not see her, discovering that God had identified her. When a life that is light-years away from God tries to find a shortcut back there are bound to be problems.

11

A superficial reading of the ensuing judgement that came upon Jeroboam's household could suggest that this had all happened simply because the family had backslidden. Hardly. God is not spiteful. The tender heart of God was the same then as it was portrayed in the parable Jesus was to tell one thousand years later as he spoke of the father out looking for, and willing to welcome, his prodigal son.

If Jeroboam's wife, and better still Jeroboam himself, had gone to the prophet in an attitude of repentance and humility few would fail to imagine the result. The Queen came in disguise, pretending to be someone else. There is only one way to come to God and, without doubt, Charlotte Elliott had it right when she wrote the lines of her hymn, *Just as I am without one plea*. As far as God is concerned, only those with an open face will ever find an open door.

The Mask before God

Perhaps the worst of all is the Mask of Spirituality. It is worn in public and private prayer when we speak to God in correct terminology about what we think are the right things imagining that we can fool Him. It is worse when, struggling to praise, the heart harbours hurt and anger, even against God, for what is considered to be unanswered prayer or a raw deal. An open face before the Lord requires that I speak to Him as I genuinely am, not as I think He thinks I should be. David spoke of 'pouring out the heart' to Him.[5] There is no eloquence in the universe that can coin a vocabulary to adequately mask from God even the weakest whisper of a wounded spirit. Why bother trying? Nothing can hide from the laser gaze of a loving God – He who 'penetrates even to dividing soul and spirit, joints and marrow; and judges the thoughts and attitudes of the heart.[6] No one is immune to the potential for mask wearing. Twentieth century Pentecostals and Restorationists may not have the liturgy and ceremonial of the historic churches but any form of worship, historic or contemporary, can be hidden behind. When the form becomes a facade the service, clouding reality, becomes little more than a smokescreen. Worship may be expressed, but it is not in spirit and truth.

Even religious observance can become a front. Tithing and faithful church attendance can never be a substitute for a real encounter with God. Few were more astute in this respect than the Pharisees but of them Jesus said, 'You are like whitewashed tombs, which look beautiful on the outside but on the inside are full of dead men's bones and everything unclean. In the same way, on the outside you appear to people as righteous but on the inside you are full of hypocrisy and wickedness.[7] Isaiah spoke strongly against those who fasted regularly and adhered to the smallest letter of the Law but in whose lives there was a clear lack of love, justice and mercy. Such people find their parallel today in those who feel the need to major on the most minor points and who will argue, at the expense of fellowship and relationship, on secondary and peripheral things. All too often trivial matters are used to mask hidden agendas. A minister friend of mine has a plaque on the wall of the office in which his various church committees meet, which declares, 'Will it increase the kingdom?' If it doesn't they refuse to allow the issue to cloud their consideration and sap their energy.

Then there is the mask of commitment – the vow too easily or unthinkingly made. It must have been quite some meeting that Ananias and his wife Sapphira attended. The apostles had been laying out the challenge that it was wrong that those who had been made one parent families because of imprisonment, persecution or bereavement should be suffering financially while others in the church were far more materially secure. They were calling for something far more than a charitable poor-box or a social security system, only radical commitment to one another would suffice. Having all things in common was the only practical solution.

If everyone in your row in a Convention or Celebration meeting has gone out to the front, it can take more courage to stay where you are than to join them. When everyone around you is promising houses, land and other possessions vow-making can become almost contagious.

Ananias and his wife nudged one another into conformity and added theirs to the volley of hands that were shooting up all over the church. It was when they got home at night that their minds began to do a slow motion action replay of the previous few hours. 'Did we really say that . . . We did?'

The plan they concocted was simple enough. It was decided that the 'For Sale' notice would go up, though only to camouflage their real intentions. When the land was sold they would withhold a percentage. Luke records the consequences. They both suffered heart attacks within three hours of each other. Early Church discipline could be bad for your health!

Why the Judgement? Was it because they did not give everything? Not at all! At the moment they withheld the true price and paid the penalty, they had given far more than most of us have done in any single act of giving. The problem was not that they had not given everything but that they had promised everything and had given less. As Peter was to put it, 'You have not lied to men but to God.'[8] Whether our promise is made through private prayer or public pronouncement, if we are to be truly open with God, the advice of Bunyan would not go amiss, 'When you pray let thy heart be without words rather than thy words be without heart.'

The Mask before one another

There has never been a time when our Western civilisation has been more image-conscious than it is today. In Great Britain, as well as in America, national leaders are not so much promoted as mass-marketed. The image of our politicians are now so highly polished that they reflect slogans, instead of policies, to the electorate.

It comes as no surprise therefore that what is projected at the top finds its way into every strata of the social order. The empty glamour and glitz of show business marketing has brought premature deaths to stars who find it hard to cope with the intolerable burden of trying to live up to their Madison Avenue packaging. By definition, a star must constantly shine brighter than anyone else. Empty people can only stay in orbit for so long. The gravitational pull of fickle public opinion drags them inevitably downwards. Too often those who once shone and scintillated come down to earth with a bang – shattered at the feet of those who once looked up to them.

Ordinary people, under nothing like the same pressure, are just as much prone to mask wearing. 'Don't look at me, look at my style', say those who are the slaves to the latest fashion. 'Don't look at me, look at my status symbols', say those who have been wooed and won by materialism. Os Guiness speaks in his book, *The Gravedigger File* of, 'Conspicuous consumption

– where spending is not so much a matter of need but of identity. Man is what he consumes.'

To ask, whether this could ever happen in the spiritual realm has long been a non-question. Already sections of the transatlantic church are paying the price for the media hype lavished upon its evangelical megastars – people living with coast to coast television programmes and wall to wall luxury. The trouble with masks is that they never stay in place long enough to be of any permanent use. They are not durable. They usually slip.

This is not to point an accusing finger unnecessarily, for everyone of us has worn a mask at some time or another. There is no one that I know who would welcome an audio-visual presentation of their every thought and deed to be broadcast universally.

One of the most common masks worn by Christians is perhaps the one we would call, 'The Big Smile'. It is worn by two different types of people. It is worn by those who labour under the illusion that it is impossible to be a real Spirit-filled Christian unless you constantly go around looking like a Cheshire cat that has been struck by lightning. It is also worn by those who feel they are dying inside but who are afraid to say so because, deep down, they feel that nobody cares enough about them to genuinely listen.

A number of years ago my wife and I were driving home from the Sunday evening service and, as so often happened on that two miles stretch from the church to the manse, found ourselves thinking of those who may have been missing from the Fellowship that day. One such person lived quite near where we lived and so we decided that we would drop in on him on our way home. When he opened the door and found us on the doorstep he was quite obviously embarrassed. It was clear that he was fit and well and we anticipated that before long he would share with us the reason for his absence. However even after I asked him directly, he resisted telling us. Feeling that he must have some underlying personal difficulty I persisted and eventually, at about 11 pm, he told me his story. It turned out that he had been dealing with some particular problem but that, in itself, was not the real issue. It emerged that on one or two occasions as I was shaking hands at the door of the church he had tried to mention his particular need to me but no sooner had I asked how he was and he had begun to speak I, while still shaking his hand and addressing him, was looking over his shoulder to greet the next person who was coming out of the church building. He had read from that situation that I was not interested in him as a person.

Some would argue the reason for his absence was petty and that if he had wanted to he could easily have telephoned me for an appointment. That aside, the fact remained that I had been at fault. We have probably all met people who ask how we are and are half way down the street before we have had the chance to answer. I learned an important lesson. I had been encouraging him to wear a mask and discouraging him, by my inattentiveness, from being totally open. Now when I greet people I endeavour to look at the only place a mask never covers, the eyes – especially when I ask how they are. Little things can matter a lot.

Another mask worn between individuals is the one which screams, 'Who needs your friendship anyway?' On one occasion a lady came to the church office to inform me that she would not be coming to our Fellowship again as the people were not friendly enough for her. One will accept criticism when it is justified but I knew for a fact that this was one of the friendliest churches that I had ever pastored to that date. They were great folk and there was no denying it. The lady who was speaking was not committed to us as a Fellowship and had in fact only been attending our church for a short time. I did not know her well but I knew her well enough to know that she was not the most friendly or approachable person I have ever met. She was the type of person who complained that no one ever spoke to her at the end of the service but who was virtually half way home herself before the closing prayer had been prayed.

Those who had spoken to her had been met with a rebuff. She was a lady who prided herself on her independent spirit. I was listening to what she was saying but knew that there must be more to her problem that what she was offering me.

As we spoke I could hear people outside working on our building. I thought that this was a cue for a question. 'Imagine', I said, 'that someone were to walk through this door now and meet you for the first time. Would you assume that they would like you immediately, dislike you immediately, or need a little time to get to know you first?'

Most people would probably choose the third option but she chose the second. It turned out that years ago she had been very badly hurt within a relationship. She vowed that she would never allow herself to be hurt like that again. Yes, she was lonely and that hurt; and yes, she would love to have friends but she had made a choice. She had to that point chosen the hurt of loneliness instead of the greater potential hurt brought about by her making herself vulnerable to love and being wounded again. Her mask of indifference and hardness was worn as a shield – as a wall to keep others out. Her difficulty had been the reverse of what she had originally suggested. The many open folk within the fellowship were slowly but surely getting behind her mask. She was becoming vulnerable and feeling the need to run. She didn't run. She stayed with us and before too long was living before the Lord and before her friends – mask free.

In every case, fear of openness in relationship stems from a basic sense of insecurity, and usually poor self image. How that could change when we realise as Billhiemer has that, 'The highest ranking angel hovering over the throne of the Most High is outranked by the most insignificant human being who has been redeemed by the blood of Christ.'[9]

The Mask within ourselves

That we find ourselves being less than honest with God, and sometimes less than open with one another, would be admitted by most people. But who would ever try to fool themselves?

Robert, (not his real name), a man in his twenties, seemed to live on a treadmill of perpetual frustration. Nothing appeared to satisfy him or fulfil him. His face reflected the tension that he felt inside. His father was entirely different. He was successful, entrepeneurial and exuded confidence. That of course was the problem. It was only when Robert gave up mask wearing – a vain attempt to emulate his father, that he came to a place of personal peace. It was at the point that he realised that God had made him as someone special and loved him as an individual that he came to understand that he was short-changing himself by striving to be a carbon-copy, a clone, of someone else.

While some wear masks as disguises and others wear masks as shields there are also those who wear masks as shelters and smokescreens. The 'I'm useless and never get anywhere' version is a case in point. It is the camouflage of the sincerely timid and also of those who are downright lazy. It is donned by those with commitment anxiety who just want to be part of the crowd – who like being in a large congregation for no other reason than that it is an excellent place to hide. Talent abounds as do jobs to be done but there are plenty of others to do them. The greatest tragedy about mask-wearing is that the false image projected to others, becomes, after a period of time, so much part of the persona that it becomes grafted onto the face itself. The actor becomes the role and, like the mega-star who comes to believe his own publicity hand-outs, the image sticks. This is what happens too when people disqualify themselves by coming to believe the poor picture that they have painted of their lives. It does not represent reality. It is not true. It is a mask.

A perfect biblical example of this is the coronation of Saul.[10] A near political disaster if ever there was one. A coronation where everything was arranged to the finest detail and where everything was in place except the King.

The people had rejected Samuel and their motive was purely one of 'image'. They had said that they wanted to be like the other nations and a prophet in simple attire was hardly the public relation and media man's dream of a national leader – even if he did carry with him the mind and the authority of God.

Saul, on the other hand, could well have been manufactured in Madison Avenue, a veritable gift to Saatchi and Saatchi. Head and shoulders taller than any other man in Israel he presented the ideal macho concept of what a king should be. Presentable he may have been, available he wasn't.

It seemed that when the tribes camped they put tents on the perimeter of the site to house all the odds and ends. It was amongst these bits and pieces that modern versions of the Bible call 'baggage' and which the King James vesion merely designates 'stuff' that the future king had chosen to conceal himself. The greatest giants become pygmies when they hide.

One cannot but help compare this giant of a man, who began at the centre of God's purposes and who ended up far outside them, with the Saul of the New Testament who, though small in stature, began far outside God's purposes and ended up at the hub of everything.

There is many a giant lurking amongst the mundane, surrounded by little things and small ambitions, who if only they would recognise what God can do with one surrendered life would discard forever the trivia and the veil of failure that accompanies it.

Those who long to fade chameleon-like into the ordinary are usually those who employ what can only be described as 'worm theology' to cement their mask in place. It can often be heard in the prayer that reminds the Lord we are 'only dust' and that we can do 'nothing of ourselves'. These are sentiments with which many of us would readily agree but it is only half of the story. It should not be forgotten that, while the previous statements are true, we have been brought from dust into Sonship and, though the flesh is a futile vehicle through which to serve God, we can 'Do all things through Him who gives us strength'[11]

It would seem that Scripture calls not only for the individual to be open faced but that the church, in its corporate expression, be similarly mask-free. The church at Sardis is a case in point.[12] Of it the Lord says, 'You have a reputation of being alive, but you are dead.' It was depending on the decaying laurels of yesterday's blessing. A 'Movement' standing still. A leadership lost. If Saul, at whom we looked earlier, was involved in Trivial Pursuit then the game that Sardis was engaged in was totally Scrabblesque – a mere playing with words. It preached cream but lived skimmed milk. In one of his books, Gordon Macdonald tells of an antique chest that once stored dynamite but now, though still displaying the sign and bearing a warning, was relegated to a shed and housed only scraps of wood.[13] Sadly, this was Sardis – a church that had more in common with the dinosaur than with dynamite. Could it have been transferred from the first century to the twentieth and from Christendom to Commerce, it would have long ago been prosecuted under the Trade Descriptions Act. As a church Sardis could be compared to the towns which are specially constructed for the filming of Westerns. Outside everything seemed normal enough, but when you looked behind it, all you saw were props and struts.

God called the attention of Sardis to the only thing that could stop the rot: repentance. This is the sole antidote to all mask-induced conditions. Coming to terms with reality. Facing things as they are. Turning from past failure and renouncing it. Finding the cleansing that comes through forgiveness. Becoming smaller but, at least, becoming real.

What was the real scandal behind Watergate and Irangate? It was not simply the planting of listening devices in one's opponents offices nor the diverting of funds to the Contra rebels. These issues seem almost lost in the labyrinth of the circumstances that were to follow. The real matter was 'cover up' – that which masked. When Adam sinned he realised that he was naked. He looked for a solution that did not involve repentance. Sardis offered God fig leaves when what He was looking for was fruit.

2: The Open Face of God

God never masks His real nature to us. Time and time again the Psalmists would speak of 'Seeking the face of God.' All the more remarkable when we realise that it is the Invisible God that can be known and the tangible idol that can't. When Moses stood before the burning bush and inquired as to whom he should tell Pharaoh had sent him, Jehovah refused to be pigeon-holed. 'Just tell him that 'I AM'' has sent you,' says God. Had Moses been introduced to any of the titles that would later have been descriptions of God's nature, whilst it may have been enlightening to him, it would have been extremely misleading for Pharaoh. 'Sun of Righteousness' would imply a Sun God as would 'Light of the world'. 'Lamb of God' would induce thoughts of a Golden Calf, neither would 'Lion of Judah' be helpful at that point in history.

'I AM' may have sounded vague to Moses but its tense, not obvious in the English translation, encompassed all that God had been, was, and ever would be. The abstract idea became concrete at the point of communion, and still does. Idols served as symbols but had no substance. They were masks behind which there was no reality. Jehovah was reality personified.

It would seem that mankind is addicted to mask making, so much so that, not satisfied in adorning themselves with such things, they have also attempted to impose such concepts upon God in order to present Him as a controlled image. Those who embrace Liberation

Theology are in danger of presenting Christ to South American village-dwellers as a left wing radical whose sole mission was the destruction of Capitalism. On the other side of the political spectrum, Christians who ally themselves with the exaggerated forms of Prosperity teaching (not to be confused with the real thing) come perilously near to capsizing the boat to the right when they seem to many to promote a doctrine in which Christ is displayed as the champion of the American Dream. It is abundantly clear that the teaching of Jesus was, and still is, radical. It is also true that many Christians need to be emancipated from a spirit of poverty. What is vital though is that the Creator is perceived in the way that He has chosen to reveal Himself and not as a reflection of his creatures' bias. It was the Puritan John Trapp who said, 'God made man in His own image and man has now made gods in his own image to get even.'

How then does God want to be 'seen'? There is a key word to be found in both the Old and New Testaments. Jeremiah asks, 'Has a nation ever changed its gods . . . but my people have exchanged their Glory for worthless idols'[1] To the church at Rome Paul writes of those who, in his day, 'Exchanged the glory of the immortal God for images.'[2] It is the glory of God in its various expressions that is the truest revelation of Jehovah.

When Moses said, 'Lord show me your Glory' God's response was, 'I will cause all my goodness to pass in front of you, and I will proclaim my Name, the Lord, in your presence.'[3] Moses understood God's glory by a revelation of the communicable attributes of God. David experienced the glory of God through the revelation of the personality of God in His creative works. God was speaking about Himself through Creation. In the nineteenth psalm he says, 'The heavens declare the glory of God; the skies proclaim the works of His hands. Day after day they pour forth speech; night after night they display knowledge. There is no speech or language where their voice is not heard. Their voice goes out into all the earth. Their words to the end of the world.'

The Apostle Paul felt that God's creative work was so articulate that its revelation alone was sufficient proof of the existence of God. To the Romans he writes, 'For since the creation of the world God's invisible qualities – His eternal power and divine nature – have been clearly seen, being understood from what he has made, so that men are without excuse.'[4]

In the Fourth Gospel John records, 'The Word became flesh and lived for a while among us. We have seen His Glory. The Glory of the one and only Son, who came from the Father, full of grace and truth.' The writer to the Hebrews says, 'The Son is the radiance of God's glory and the exact representation of his being.' But perhaps the most graphic and vivid insight into the way in which God wishes to reveal Himself through his glory is seen in Paul's second letter to the Corinthians, 'For God . . . made His light to shine in our hearts to give us the light of the knowledge of the glory of God in the *face of Jesus Christ*.'[5]

All that was understood of God in the Old Testament is revealed in Christ. The goodness that Moses saw is embodied in Him. As far as Creation is concerned, He is the origin of all things.[6] As far as power was concerned this was seen in His miraculous works. Significantly, at the marriage in Cana in Christ's first recorded miracle John records, 'He thus revealed his glory, and his disciples put their faith in Him.'[7]

God had worn no masks through Old Testament times and in the New Testament reveals the tangible presence of Deity. Not masked, though 'veiled in flesh'. His flesh becomes a protective screen else mankind would not be able to cope, let alone stand before, the raw Glory of Almighty God – a transformer stepping down the voltage of heaven for our benefit.

It is the next phase of God's revealed glory that becomes the most challenging. In John 17 we are allowed to eavesdrop upon Jesus speaking to His Father. What the disciples heard must have rooted them to the spot. They, like us, understood how God had been manifested in Old Testament times, and seemed fully aware of the One they were currently serving. But what Jesus was saying now must have seemed to them to be almost unbelievable. 'I have given them the glory that you gave me . . .'[8] It was now their responsibility to reveal to the world what God was like. Christ was returning to the Father. They, and the Believers who would follow them, would now constitute the body of Christ upon Earth. He had promised that, when He went, He would send the Holy Spirit. They were sure that they would need Him. They would wait and wait until He came and eventually, on the day of Pentecost, He did.

The Apostle Paul would later use the phrase in his prayer for the Christians in Ephesus, 'To Him be Glory in the church.'[9] It became now, more than ever, vital that those who had been ordained to reflect His Glory remained totally mask-free. Isaiah had prophesied, 'Arise and shine for your light has come and the glory of the Lord arises on you. See darkness covers the earth and thick darkness is over the peoples but the Lord rises on you. Nations will come to your light and kings to the brightness of your dawn.'[10] It was clear that this Glory had commended his love to a lost world through His death. His body on Earth were now called to reveal His nature to the world by their lives. Paul lost no opportunity in making this clear to individuals and churches alike. He knew well from his own experience how stone-cold theology in isolation could be. He exhorts Timothy not only to take heed to his doctrine but also to his manner of life. Christ was to return, not just for a bride that was morally pure and doctrinally sound, He was coming for a beautiful bride. She would be not only attractive to Him but gloriously attractive to the world. Not just a beauty that would turn heads but one which would turn many hearts towards the Bridegroom. Asaph the psalmist had it right when he said, 'Out of Zion, perfect in beauty, God shines forth.'[11]

When the Greeks came to Philip and said, 'Sir, we would like to see Jesus' the solution was simple enough. Today, when the question is asked, a reply should be able to be, 'Would you wait a moment please? I'll find you a Christian.'

There is hardly a child in Sunday School who could not harmonise the two apparently contradictory statements of Jesus where He says on one hand that He is the light of the world and on another occasion, of His disciples, that they were the light of the world. The analogy is usually drawn between the sun which we say is the light by day and the moon which we refer to as the light by night. In a sense that is true but in another it is not. Everyone knows that the moon has no innate capacity for shining. The feet of modern man have stood on its rocky surface. The moon shines only as it reflects the light source of the sun. Its value is solely as a reflector. So too the Christian. Of ourselves there is nothing in us that would recommend us to God nor man. Our total usefulness as disciples is in direct proportion to our ability to radiate the beauty of Jesus into a dark world. It is therefore essential that nothing at all must come between us and the light. Communion must be completely unhindered. The mirror must remain unmarred. Understanding that we 'get to be like the people we live with' and basking in His presence takes precedence over forever bringing Him the shopping list of our petitions. The longer you spend in the sun the more like the Son you become.

The theology of all this is encapsulated in Paul's second letter to the Corinthians, 'And we, who with unveiled faces all reflect the Lord's glory, are being transformed into his likeness with ever-increasing glory, which comes from the Lord, who is the Spirit.'[12]

Some would put great importance on the architectural grandeur of church buildings, the academic qualifications of their pastoral staff, size of congregation, or musical ministry. Some of these things have their rightful and important place but, in reality, the sole attraction of the Church and Body of Christ is the degree to which it effectively, and efficiently, reflects the Glory of God.

3: Open Ears

In the days when the communications industry was rather less dominated by the passing of digital information along glass fibre-optic cable and rather more a case of deciphering dots and dashes, an advertisement was placed for a well paid and influential post. It was for a person who was an expert in transmitting and receiving Morse Code.

Hundreds of folk applied, and the preliminary interviews over, the short list was narrowed down to just six people. They were asked to meet the senior personnel manager of the company at a hotel and were requested to assemble in the lobby awaiting their call to the interview room.

The reception area was not greatly different from many other hotel lobbies of the era. Large dralon sofas, chairs – some matching, others of the stylish wicker variety. A long dark-wood desk with brass accessories dominated the room and over the tannoy floated music that, like audible wallpaper, blended into the background.

Dispensing with hats and coats, the final six were introduced to each other, and began to weigh up their opposition as they waited to be called. Where they had been educated, what qualifications and experience they each had, dominated their conversation.

Within five or six minutes they noticed that one of their company was missing. It was evident that he had not just slipped away temporarily, for his hat and coat were gone from the stand. The reason, they all concluded, was obvious. He could not face the competition. It was too stiff. He had left to save face, to save himself the embarrassment of being turned down.

Further conjecture was halted by the arrival of the personnel manager. The six were so busy, wondering who would be the first to be interviewed that they were not ready for his opening remark.

'Thank you for coming, interviews are over, you may now leave.' Over? They had not even begun. But they had – whilst they were comparing themselves with one another and assessing their prospects. As suitcase-carrying porters passed with the luggage of new arrivals and ex-residents, and waiters strutted about their business, and with the music still playing; behind the music was something that all but one of them had missed. It was the soft staccato of a morse code operator summoning the first interviewee to the appropriate room.

Amongst all that was going on, amongst all the legitimate things that vied for their attention, none of those left in the lobby had been sensitive enough to pick up the message directed at them. The post had gone to the applicant with an open ear.

God looks for, and uses, the person who will listen. The one who can hear His voice above the static of every thing else that stakes its claim for undivided attention. Someone has said that an average person can be the recipient of no less than two thousand messages in the course of a single day. They range from the obvious and necessary demands of the home, wife, children, of business, the telephone, colleagues, superiors. They encompass the more subliminal calls from advertising, placards and signs such as 'No Entry, 'One Way' or 'Keep off the Grass'.

It's a noisy world – yet God still wants to speak. He longs and loves to share His heart and mind with His

Creation. Though many different messages were transmitted to the very different Seven Churches of Revelation one thing acted as a common denominator to them all and it was, 'He who has an ear, let him hear what the Spirit says to the churches.'[1]

It was a number of years before I realised that snake charming was mentioned in the Bible. Though I must have read Psalm 58 many times before, the fourth and fifth verses had never really captured my attention. It spoke of a people who were 'Like the Cobra that has stopped its ears that will not heed the tune of the charmer.' It was perhaps this that inspired Shakespeare to pen in *Troilus and Cressida*, 'Pleasure and revenge have ears more deaf than adders to the voice of any true decision.'

The snake charmer was the busker of Old Testament times. He plied his trade wherever crowds gathered: the market place, beside busy streets, near to tourist attractions. A consistent crowd was great news for the piper but not a little exhausting for the snake. At the best of times snakes are not known for their sense of hearing but, even so, once the pipe begins to play the tune becomes irresistible. The reptile moves and gyrates to its haunting call, and bobs and sways as the hypnotic pipe moves from side to side. The Psalmist intimates that, were it possible, the only way that the cobra would be able to resist would be to block out the playing of the charmer. Only then could it resist its call.

The greatest charmer in the universe is the Holy Spirit. Time and time again He is described as the One who draws and woos the Bride of Christ to her celestial Bridegroom. The Church of Jesus Christ is comprised of millions from different races, cultures, even periods of history: people who, though diverse in many ways, have all been, without exception 'drawn with cords of love', to the Saviour. They have been attracted by the music of grace, a sound which many Christians consider irresistible to those who will listen.

Though the call to salvation is the first of this kind that we hear it is certainly not the last. The call to service follows, and sometimes to sacrifice and suffering. The call to discipleship and holiness is also indelibly written into the contract. As they say in America – it goes with the territory.

Why do Christians close their ears when God is speaking? On a human level is is rude, on a spiritual level it would seem almost inexcusable. The answer is simple enough: listening leads to responding and responding means change.

Prejudice and deafness

The book of Acts records Stephen's speech as he stood before the Sanhedrin. He opens up his message with the words, 'Brothers listen to me' and as he spoke about Abraham, Joseph, Moses, they did. It was what he said later that would cause communication to break down. Having accused them of resisting the Holy Spirit, betraying and murdering the Messiah – obviously not a man to mince words – they threw him out and prepared to stone him. Even though they were violently angry they were still listening. That was until he looked toward heaven and said, 'Look, I see heaven open and the Son of Man standing on the right hand of God.' People can stand almost everything except people who have visions. Discussion on theological issues may display only that someone knows their Bible more than you. Visions imply that someone is experiencing the Lord in a deeper way. Some of us, if we are honest, can find that pretty unpalatable medicine.

The physical response of the Sanhedrin is very significant indeed, 'At this they covered their ears and, yelling at the top of their voices, they all rushed at him, dragged him out of the city and began to stone him . . .'[2] They had done two things to block out the message and the final murderous act was an attempt to block out the messenger. Had Stephen been the messenger they would have succeeded. He wasn't. The Holy Spirit was speaking through him. The narrative says so.

'The word of God is not bound' was a statement that would be uttered years later by the young man, who Luke mentions almost in passing, as the one at whose feet they left their clothes.

Stephen had told them earlier that they were stiff-necked, with uncircumcised hearts and ears. In fact it would appear that their hearing was not too bad at all. It was their listening that was proving a problem. Though the fact that Jesus was indeed the Messiah had been clearly revealed they would not accept it. Truth had been unable to pass the violent picket line of their own prejudice.

This scene reminds us of the one in which Gallileo is hauled up before the Inquisition for daring to proclaim the heresy that the Earth revolved around the sun. The Interrogation over and having received the sternest of rebukes he leaves the room with the parting shot, 'But it moves just the same.' Truth is incontrovertible. Facts are never affected by our unwillingness to listen to them.

My first pastoral appointment after leaving theological college was to a small town in South Wales. The congregation was not at all large but it seemed that virtually everyone was talented in one way or another. It certainly had a higher than usual proportion of people with a musical ministry. I was fortunate. I designed the Gospel service to run like a smooth machine. Musicians knew exactly the place they were in the programme and when to move to the microphone. The style was slick, predictable and I was proud of it.

It was during this period that one of the men in the church came to me and asked if he could have a word with me about the Sunday evening service. I said of course that he could and made a mental note to look suitably humble when the inevitable accolade of appreciation came.

'Pastor,' he began, and then hesitated – I assumed at a loss for which of a galaxy of superlatives to use. 'Pastor, I feel that the only difference between our Sunday night service and the London Palladium is that those taking part don't go round on a revolving platform at the end.'

I concluded that, at best, he was a little off colour and, at worse, backslidden. Purposefully maintaining eye-contact so not as to appear ruffled, I inquired as to what he was really trying to say.

He spoke, among other things, of a more unstructured meeting, open worship and the exercise of spiritual gifts. My clear retort was that he could find all of those things in the morning service but on Sunday evening such things would only serve to confuse the unconverted people who would be attending. His suggestion, to my mind, was completely out of place.

It was a couple of years later that I left that Fellowship and moved to a church in the Midlands and during the opening months of my pastorate we planned a major Crusade. A great deal of money was spent on this outreach, even by today's standards. The Evangelist was booked and as I stood on the platform on the opening night I could see that the place was packed – not just with Christians but with a higher proportion of unsaved people than I had ever seen in a Crusade meeting before. I concluded that our high profile advertising had obviously paid off.

A short way into the meeting I handed over to the Evangelist. I could not believe it. To my dismay he suggested to the congregation that we spend a period of time in open worship – in an Evangelistic service! I looked out at the non-Christians in the congregation for what I was convinced would be the last time. Not only was I sure that I would never see them again but I had a constant picture in my mind, like a video on a loop, of money pouring down a drain. I could not have been more wrong.

We saw the people come back night after night. Many of them were Born Again during those meetings. Later I found out that when they had heard the preacher speak of a God who who was alive their initial response was, 'Well, he would say that wouldn't he.' They knew that that was what he was there for and, as far as they were concerned, was also what he was paid for. It was when they looked and saw the people around them worshipping, some with hands raised and others not, that the impact took effect. These people were clearly relating to someone that they knew to be alive. That night they had been listening not just to one message but were surrounded by scores of simultaneous sermons. Worship had become Evangelistic.

No one could have come to Christ without the clear declaration of the Gospel message but in that service I realised that signs can sometimes precede the preaching of the Word as well as follow it.

I could not help but remember the man who had spoken to me those few years earlier. Some time later when returning to the church in Wales to minister I made sure that I got to see him. There were things that I needed to say to him.

Prejudiced people do not always have an axe to grind or a chip on their shoulder. I have met many folk since who really believe that they are open to God but who leave you with the clear impression that God has revealed to them the last word on everything that needs to be communicated. I know the feeling. Though what is the point of pretending to be listening if really, deep down, you do not believe that there is anything left to be said?

Guilt and Deafness

It is a cause of amazement to many that God would want to communicate with His creation at all. Yet He does. No just to spiritual and national leaders but to men and women, boys and girls. To all of us. If we fail to be attentive we are the losers. If church leaders fail to hear what God is saying then the consequences stretch much further.

In the Old Testament dispensation God choose to speak to Prophets and to Priests who in turn relayed the mind of the Lord to the people. Most folk in those days heard from God second hand. If a man like Eli, for example, was not listening then a whole Nation would be affected. If he could not hear then, effectively, the whole country went deaf. On one occasion in the life of Israel this actually happened. At that time the Scriptures record 'In those days the word of the Lord was rare.'[3]

Hophni and Phineas, two sons of Eli and both priests, were living way out of line. The catalogue of their crimes were almost beyond belief and, what is more, they were getting away with it. Eli had rebuked them on more than one occasion but had failed to re-train them. He was aware that it was his responsibility to stop what they were doing and put them out of office. He refused to. There were a number of reasons for this but one of them was that Eli personally profited from some of the things that they were involved in.[4]

God had spoken so often about this to Eli that it got to the point that whenever the man would come to seek the mind of God on behalf of the people the moment he closed his eyes he would get an action replay of his own disobedience. The result was inevitable. He stopped praying. He went deaf because listening was proving far too uncomfortable.

What was to happen next was to become one of the classic Sunday School lessons of all time. And what a story: the most influential and mature spiritual leader in the land by-passed in favour of a small inexperienced lad whose highest pinnacle of responsibility up to that point had been to function as the Temple cleaner.

I wonder how Eli felt, when Samuel had come to his room for the third time that night, telling him that should the Lord call again he was to say, 'Speak Lord for our servant is listening.' What an incredible irony.

Samuel had been willing to listen but he was clearly reluctant to pass the message on. The subject matter had been not for him at all but for Eli. It was what God had been trying to get through to him for months. If God can not get through to us on one line, because of the screeching static of neglected responsibility, He will sometimes put the receiver down and try again on another – though His Spirit will not always strive with man. The day may come when the plug is pulled.

Circumstances can arise when our deafness becomes contagious and, of all people, God is the One who catches it. The Bible says so. This problem lies at the heart of many things that are wrongly labelled, 'Unanswered Prayer' when they should more correctly be marked as 'Unheard Prayer'. The Psalmist says, 'If I regard iniquity in my heart the Lord will not hear me.'[5] The writer of the book of Proverbs says, 'If anyone turns a deaf ear to the Law, even his prayers are detestable.'[6]

Deafness with God is never a negative trait, it is always a positive act. It is not that He cannot hear it is simply that He chooses not to listen. When we turn to Him in repentance, for it is only that that will effectively shringe our ears, it is not that He forgets our sins – He just chooses to remember them no more.

I knew a lady on one occasion who requested prayer at the end of a church service. A visiting speaker was present who had never met the lady before and who had no previous knowledge of her. She expained that she suffered from a nervous condition the symptoms of which manifested themselves in a number of ways, not least in a painful stomach disorder. He was about to pray when the Lord revealed to him that, some years ago, this lady had had a violent disagreement with a former friend. This relationship had never been resolved and repaired even though the Lord had pointed out the need for this to her on a number of occasions. Her physical condition was the result of the spiritual condition. As a result it was not only pride that she was having difficult in swallowing. He confronted the lady with this revelation as gently as possible and discovered the facts to be true. It was clear that as she was not hearing God's plea for reconciliation He was not hearing her request for healing. This was not the act of a petulant God it was the response of One who cannot contradict Himself. God refuses to build on foundations that are shaky or on premises that are false. It was not another prayer that she needed. It was merely a simple act of submission to what

God had been saying to her. A myriad of unheralded and unnoticed miracles emanate from life-styles lived quietly in obedience to the will of God.

The epistle of James, again in the context of healing, encompassing all guilt-related spiritual hearing difficulties says, 'Confess you sins to each other and pray for each other so that you may be healed. The prayer of a righteous man is powerful and effective.'[7]

Commitment and deafness

Everything that God says demands a response. Every message ends with RSVP. That is what makes listening so demanding for us. This is nowhere more graphically illustrated than in the acount of the Apostle Paul's trial before Felix. Luke records, 'He sent for Paul and listened to him as he spoke about faith in Christ Jesus. As Paul discoursed on righteousness, self-control and the judgement to come, Felix was afraid and said, 'That's enough for now! You may leave. When I find it convenient, I will send for you.'[8] Such convenient seasons are about as rare as a snowflake in a furnace. Felix had no problem with faith preaching. That was palatable. A call to holiness though pin-pointed too many no-go areas in his life. The barricades went up. Selective hearing and convenient deafness are two sides of the same coin.

Hell-fire preaching has always had more than its fair share of a bad press. Yet it has to be said that sometimes the criticism has been valid. Fierce-faced ranters calling down the wrath of God on a sinful world have all too often been the dispensers of a callous and love-less preaching. The message may be as true as the judgement is justified but unless the mixture is ignited with the spark plug of compassion the evangelistic engine will always fail to fire. The same Jesus that took cords to drive the money changers out of the Temple is also the one who shed rivers of tears over Jerusalem. He wept before he whipped.

The story is told of two young Salvation Army officers in the formative days of their Movement who were assigned to an area but saw hardly any success. In their frustration they wrote to General Booth telling him that they felt that they had done all that could be done. They had worked, witnessed and warned of a judgement to come. What more could they do? The message they received in response was composed of only two short words. It read, 'Try tears'. It turned out that that was to be the key that opened up the door to a great harvest for them. One of the songs of ascents says, 'Those who sow in tears will reap with songs of joy. He who goes out weeping, carrying seeds to sow, will return with songs of joy, carrying sheaves with him.'[9] It is sometimes said that Evangelism fails in some places due to the innate and peculiar difficulties of the area. Could it be that the hardness is not always in the ground but sometimes in the sower? Hell can't be preached without heart. In the same way, heaven cannot be spoken of outside the context of a total commitment to the Lordship of Jesus.

One of the signs of the end times is that of a society, 'That would not put up with sound doctrine. Instead, to suit their own desires, they will gather around them a great number of teachers to say what their itching ears want to hear. They will turn their ears away from the truth and turn aside to myths.'[10] If that is not an example of selective hearing then nothing is.

We saw earlier how God would not allow himself to be portrayed as a controlled image. Neither will He allow His Gospel to be so portrayed. He is indivisible from His Word. Heaven cannot be understood without

41

Hell in the same way that, for the Christian, true happiness cannot be experienced without holiness. Similarly, material prosperity becomes a spiritual orphan if not related to social responsibility. Only itching ears hear differently.

When Jesus raised the dead He drew the crowds. When He suggested His disciples should take up their cross and follow Him His statistics were slimmer. Hard words are not heard well. John's Gospel records that on such occasions, 'From this time many of His disciples turned back and no longer followed him.' Of these people Jesus Himself says, 'Though hearing they do not hear or understand.'[11]

The Ear Test

I once had occasion to go to see an Ear Specialist and have an ear test. A pair of headphones were connected to a simple apparatus that transmitted a wide range of frequencies at various levels of sound. The person conducting the exercise stood behind me out of view, so that I could not see when he was changing the dials, and he monitored my response in the form of a graph as I indicated to him the range of sounds that my ears were able to receive. The reason for all this was because deafness can be narrowed down to particular frequencies. For example, someone may have good hearing at high and low frequencies but have difficulty with those in the middle range – the part covered by normal conversational speech.

There is a clear parallel too in the spiritual realm. Some folk find it easy to hear a call to personal commitment and even service but may have difficulty listening to God in other areas of their life. We have taken time to look at a number of things that can cause spiritual deafness. Some of them we might identify with and others may not be quite so pertinent. Perhaps it is time for a sound check. If we conduct the examination ourselves then of course it is possible to cheat. If, on the other hand, we ask the Holy Spirit to put the auriscope to our ears our results will be far more accurate. Let us look at three particular frequencies and see how we fare.

1. *How well can we hear correction, rebuke and discipline?*

I have come to think that pulpits and lecterns have an almost supernatural quality about them. At least it seems so sometimes. Imagine for a moment a preacher delivering a message about relationships or family life. See him waxing eloquent about the operation of the fruit of the Spirit in the home. Then for a moment pan the camera from the pulpit to the congregation. Catch their expressions. Watch their reactions. It seems that they are drawing the sermon material from him by their supportive mannerisms. You can almost read in the eyes of fathers, mothers, parents, the words 'Preach it, Pastor, preach it – that's just the kind of thing my partner and children need to hear.'

Now wait for a while as the message ends, the closing period of worship terminates and the benediction is pronounced. Watch as the preacher passes the magic lectern and approaches a young man in the front row.

'Hey, Bob I wonder if I could have a word with you. I noticed that you were responding positively when I was sharing some of those things a few moments ago. Bob, can I be really open with you?

'Why Pastor of course you can.'

'Well Bob, I've been just a little concerned about the way you have been treating your wife in public just recently. Now I know you may only mean those remarks in fun but I'm really coming to feel that she's beginning to take them to heart.'

'Now come on Pastor, hold on, what gives you the right to . . .'

And that from a man who only moments earlier was hanging on the preacher's every word. Did the pulpit really make the difference? Or was it more likely that there was a hearing deficiency on what we might call the 'head to head' frequency. Put another way it is expressed, 'I can't hear you if you get too close.'

Given that all spiritual leaders be they Pastors, Elders, House Group leaders, Sunday School teachers, will have one day to stand before God and give an answer not only for their own lives but also for those that have come under their leadership it is more than a little important that they, and those who follow them, have open ears.'[12]

One incident in my pastoral life will always stand out in my mind. I was conducting a Sunday morning service and something that took place during the open worship served to spoil the flow of the meeting. I approached the person responsible at the end of the service, a man in his early thirties, and pointed this out to him and explained my feelings to him as gently as I could. As I drove my car home through the city that Sunday I could not help wondering just how he would take it. Returning to the church building for the evening service I saw him standing at the door. He wanted to have a word with me straight away – as there was something, he said, that he just had to say. I confess that I anticipated confrontation but what he actually wanted to say was this, 'I just want to say thank you, Pastor, for loving me enough to tell me the truth.' I considered that to be about the biggest compliment I have ever been given. Whatever else he needed to learn that day – listening was not one of them.

2. *How teachable am I?*

To some a good teacher is defined as a person who confirms their own prejudices. To others a good teacher is a description of someone who causes them to evaluate their position in the light of the Scriptures. Traditions and forms change: only doctrines are eternal. It is biblical revelation that is the Believer's highest court of appeal. We will look later in the chapter on the 'Open Mind' to see how this affects our attitudes to change.

One of the most poignant pictures of openness is expressed by the prophet Hosea. Speaking to Israel he says these words, 'Sow for yourself righteousness, reap the fruit of unfailing love, and break up your unploughed ground; for it is time to seek the Lord, until He comes and showers righteousness on you.'[13]

The imagery he uses is significant. He asks Israel to consider a field with great harvest potential. Beneath its surface are all the minerals and trace elements to create an environment conducive to fruitfulness. Above it are rains that are ready to pour. There is only one problem. The ground is unbroken. It is unploughed. Were the rains to fall now they would only have a superficial effect. The top soil would only be marginally affected. There would be no deep work. Were the refreshing floods to flow and hit hardness the waters would dissipate and be lost.

Hosea called for the plough, a cutting instrument, to come and break up the earth's hard surface. Now when the torrents fell the water would be sure to do the ground good.

The essence of being teachable is the ability to continue listening when what is being transmitted to us appears to 'cut across' what we have always thought. We are required to retain a sense of objectivity, to weight the evidence, to examine things not in the unreliable rays of our own preconceptions but under the laser light of the Word of God.

I received this morning a letter from a young friend of mine who is at University. In it he tells me of a meeting that he attended in a local church. He says, 'I found some of the things that were said quite new to me. It was not at all what I had been used to, but then of course I could be wrong. I will need to pray about it and think the matter through.' That is what I would have expected of him. It is what God expects of all of us.

The Romans had an agricultural instrument that consisted of a long cylindrical object pulled by oxen to which jagged pieces of metal were attached. They called it the Tribulum. God calls His cutting instrument Tribulation. Yet he never cuts to wound He only cuts to heal. Suffering is sometimes the only way that God can get through to us.

C. S. Lewis once said, 'God whispers to us in our pleasures yet shouts to us in our pain. Pain is God's megaphone to rouse a deaf world.' Job said, 'God has made my heart soft for the Almighty troubleth me'[14] David said, 'Before I was afflicted I went astray but now I obey your word.'[15]

I well remember at one point of my ministry, 'running my church' – a telling phrase – as if everything depended on me. Though I may not have admitted it at the time, so many of the plans and programmes I was involved in were being initiated by me and offered to God for rubber-stamping as if He were some kind of cosmic civil servant.

When one day I lay, seriously ill, in a hospital ward it was amazing how the acoustics changed and my ear became more finely tuned. All at once I was hearing things God had been trying to tell me for a long time. It was not me and my ministry that was at the centre of the universe: God was. The tribulum was cutting across the surface of my view of my personal field. It was uncomfortable, it was therapeutic; He was continuing to teach me and I was beginning to learn. Of course, if I had been listening more closely in the first place God would never have had to shout.

One of the greatest listening verses in the Old Testament is found in the second book of Samuel. It is a great Evangelistic text too. It says, 'God . . . devises ways so that a banished person may not remain estranged from Him.'[16]

For Jonah, it meant stormy circumstances and eventual incarceration in the great fish. For the Prodigal Son, financial impoverishment was the vehicle that was to drive him home. For Saul on the Damascus road, physical blindness became the doorway to spiritual enlightenment. Contemporary Jonahs and present-day prodigals continually discover that is far better to stay locked on to the Divine Navigator rather than going our own way, getting lost, and coming home on a third class ticket of distress. No one knows better than God how to grab our attention.

Brokennes is not a disqualification for service it is the only criteria for a credential. Even God cannot fill with Himself those that are full of themselves. We discard and jettison broken things. Broken people are the only people God can really use. Peter, smashed on the anvil of his own failure was later filled with the Holy Spirit. God flooded into the vacuum created by a vacated ego. Breakdowns are sometimes breakthroughs – especially when it is God that does the breaking.

3. *Can we hear love and forgiveness?*
Surely everyone can. I wish it were true. I have met many who are able to hear acutely the faintest sound of

chastening but are stone deaf to the loudest expression of love. Some will go so far as to invent sounds that are not there and imagine that criticism is being transmitted when it is not. Condemnation confirms their battered image of themselves. Love is alien and strange because they cannot see themselves as lovable. Some can believe in theological mercy and can believe that through grace God has forgiven them, yet they cannot forgive themselves. God has a word for such people. He longs to show them that his everlasting arms that surround them are not just strong. They are also warm. Children have a need not only to be chastised at certain times, they also have the need to to be cuddled. So too the children of God.

Coming to understand the love of God not just theologically but also experientially is one thing. Being able to receive love and appreciation from fellow Christians can be quite another. We have seen previously that hearing problems can spring from an inadequate view of God or a poor view of self. It can also emanate from a wrong view of the biblical concept of humility.

My mind goes back to a convention at which I once spoke. I came to the microphone immediately following a lady who had ministered in song. Her singing had been a tremendous blessing and had brought the congregation to an ideal attitude of openness to God just before I was to deliver the message that I had felt that the Lord had for the people that night. I made a mental note that, should our paths cross after the service had concluded, I would thank her for the contribution she had made to the meeting. It so happened that I did see her and I did express my appreciation. I was not prepared however for what was to happen next. It seemed like an eternity but could only have been a minute or so that she went on about the fact that all she wanted to do was 'hide behind the cross' and I should 'not look at her but look at Jesus'. I told her that I think I understood what she was trying to say but all I wanted to say was 'Thank you'. Unfortunately she was unable to hear it. To her, receiving appreciation was somehow unspiritual. What a pity. I am sure it would not have done her any harm if she had listened. In my experience, far more Christians die of broken hearts than die of swollen egos.

4: Open Eyes

Joe and Mavis were home at last. He had spent a hard day at the office and she had been busy around the house. Dinner over and dishes done all that remained now was for them to settle down to a quiet night in front of the television. It was already dark outside and the intermittent lashings of wind and rain against the window only served to reinforce their cosy sense of well-being.

Peter and Wendy who lived next door had much in common with their neighbours. Both of them had been out at work that day. The difference was that Peter and Wendy were Christians. As their car pulled away from the kerb at around 7:15 pm, Joe said to his wife the same thing that he seemed to say to her every Tuesday at this time of night to the accompaniment of the vehicle accelerating through the gears, 'Well they're off to church again; and on a night like this too. Honestly, I really can't see why they find all that kind of thing so important, can you Mavis?' Mavis was not listening. With the television papers in one hand, and remote control in the other, Mavis was preoccupied with other things.

Two statements that Joe had said were true. The first was that he was honest and the second was that he could not see. Physically he had twenty-twenty vision. Materially, he had a teletext television. Spiritually he was blind.

The Apostle Paul put it like this, 'The god of this age has blinded the minds of unbelievers, so that they cannot see the light of the gospel of the glory of Christ, who is the image of God.'[1] Peter paints the other side of the picture by portraying those who had come to Christ as people who have been, 'Called out of darkness into His wonderful light.'[2]

Although our emphasis is on the open eye, sight is of no use without light. The Christian needs to possess both the capacity to see and the willingness to receive revelation when it is given. It is one thing to be enlightened it is another thing altogether to 'abide in the light'.

When the blind man from Bethsaida was brought to Jesus and the Lord had laid His hands on him, Jesus asked him how he was. He replied to the effect that he was better but still could not distinguish men from trees. When Jesus laid hands on him again the response was that now he could see everything clearly. God's desire for us is not just that we are able to see but that we are able to see clearly. Revelation comes to those with open eyes. On the mount of transfiguration the gospel writer notes for us that it was only when the disciples were 'fully awake' that they saw His glory. In other words, God is looking for a people who are looking.

When we thumb through the medical records of biblical characters we find more than a few who suffered from spiritual eye problems.

Short-sightedness

This is the ability to see things close to us but a great difficulty in distinguishing objects that are any distance away. On a spiritual level, this optical malady affects not only individuals but, on some occasions, many thousands of people all at one time. Physically, it occurs when images are focussed on the front of the retina rather than on it. Spiritually, it can be a contagious disease. Unless an immunity is quickly built up it can be caught when coming into contact with others of a similar disposition. We will see that even folk with the very best eyes of faith can be afflicted with shortsightedness, though sometimes only for a relatively short period.

No one would ever think that Abraham could ever have contracted the virus, but in fact there was a time when he did. It was his father, Terah, who first had the idea to leave Ur of the Chaldeans to travel to Canaan but when he got to Haran he settled for what he could see rather than what could have been his.[3] As we shall see, this is ever a classic symptom of shortsightedness. Abraham had the vision and faith to move right out of the whole vicinity of Ur and move into the promises of God – not bad at sevety five years of age. Canaan may have been a long way over the hill, but he wasn't. Unfortunately, by the time he got to Egypt the virus struck him too. All he was able to see at that moment was a beautiful wife by his side and assumed that if the Egyptians saw her too they would take her and kill him. He immediately 'lost sight' of the promise God had given him only a short time earlier, 'To your offspring I will give this land.'[4] 'Descendents' were too far away to recognise. All he could see was the current prospect of an early grave. Even great men can be shortsighted sometimes. Later the virus was to affect his son Isaac who would do the same thing in the very same circumstances as his father.[5] It would appear from this account that there was an hereditary factor in spiritual eye conditions, at least in Old Testament times.

Esau presents us with one of the clearest examples of shortsightedness. Esau had the great macho image of a hairy hunter whilst his brother Jacob was portrayed as someone who preferred to stay at home in the kitchen, cooking. Given that his father was one of the most wealthy men alive and that, as the first-born he would be likely to get not only a double portion of the material inheritance but also the principal blessing spiritually, the swap he made for the bowl of stew certainly cost him dearly.

It proved to be the second most expensive meal in the history of the universe. The meal with the biggest price tag was the apple which Adam took in preference to all the blessings of paradise. The deal that Esau struck affected him alone. The terms that Adam negotiated affected all mankind. Adam goes down on record as not only the first man on Earth but also the most shortsighted.

These men epitomise the contemorary existentialist passion for the 'here and now'. 'Live now and pay later' refers not only to the consumerist passion of the credit card generation but also to the sexual consumerism that wills our world to close its eyes to future consequential loss of either virginity, dignity or both.

No less than eight of the ten spies who explored Canaan turned out to be shortsighted. This was something of a pity in that you expect spies, of all people, to have at least reasonably good eye sight. On their mission they would have, doubtless, paid their respects at the field of Macpelah as they went through Hebron. It was there that the Patriarchs had been buried. Perhaps, while there, their minds went back to the time when Abraham routed the armies of the five kings with only three hundred and eighteen men – but of course that was over six hundred years ago. None of them would want to argue with the victory that Abraham had seen then. Their problem was with the giants of Anak that they could see now. The shortsightedness with which Abraham had once suffered said in effect, 'God promises to be powerful tomorrow but today is a different story.' The shortsightedness of the spies said the opposite, 'God was powerful yesterday but today is a different story.' These spies were the prototype pessimists and are paralleled today with those who talk about the blessing of days gone by but fail to see God's hand at work in the times in which we live. Doubt is ever the darkroom in which negatives are developed.

If anyone were to doubt that this malady is contagious then they should look at what was to happen next. A whole nation was contaminated by the negative, 'majority report'.

These were the people, a whole generation of them, who had looked at the future through the eyes of the spies rather than through the eye of faith. As a result they perished in a desert. The post mortem published in the book of Hebrews tells us that the cause of death was lack of vision.[6] Shortsightedness, uncorrected, can kill. Ask any driving examiner. Without vision people perish.

The Bible gives an account of someone who was healed of shortsightedness in an instant and was able to see beyond his former limited perspective through into a totally new dimension and vista of faith. When Aram was at war with Israel the servant of Elisha went out early in the morning to find that the city was completely surrounded. In distress he called to his master, 'O my lord, what shall we do?' In response Elisha prayed, 'O Lord, open his eyes so that he may see'. The prayer was answered and the young servant saw the solution as well as the problem. He was given faith that saw beyond the natural limitation of human sight. That is exactly what faith is – the 'evidence of things not seen'. Remarkable things are said of Moses in this respect, 'By faith he left Egypt not fearing the king's anger; he persevered because he saw Him who is invisible.' You can hardly get better vision than that.[7]

Some would say, and I would have to agree with them, that real faith consisted in Elisha's servant having confidence in God without the supernatural evidence that was made available to him. After all, the army of God did not materialise just because he saw them. They were there all the time. I believe that faith to endure is, very often, of a higher quality than the faith that brings an instant deliverance.

When the disciples were caught in the storm and thought that they were going to drown their immediate reflex was to run to Jesus in the crisis. One would have imagined that they would have been commended for the action, but, on the contrary, Jesus rebuked them later for being of little faith. They had forgotten in the midst of the maelstrom that Jesus had earlier said to them, 'Let us go on over to the other side'. He said they were going over: they felt they were going down. Their shortsightedness saw only as far as the side of the boat. They made precisely the same mistake that Abraham had made. The promise was beyond the horizon of their spiritual sight. To have had the 'peace of God', a phrase we use all to glibly sometimes, they should have had the same peace that Jesus had. He was asleep and resting and they were awake and frantic.

Most of us have been just where they were at some time in our lives. They, and we, should have learned from Daniel's experience. What would you have done having been thrown into the lion's den? Most of us, clambering to our feet as quickly as possible, would have immediately begun to pray – for the death of the lions. In effect we would have been praying for the immediate threat to be removed so that we could be at peace. That is not what Daniel did. If he had have done it would still have been a great miracle and, if it had happened today, he would have banner headlines in every Christian periodical and guest appearances on every Bible week platform in the land. I can see it now, 'Come and see the man who struck the lions dead!' Great headlines, but Daniel could see further than the instant miracle. Not only did he not pray such a prayer but was able to rest that night – with the potential threat still present. He probably even used one of those furry forms as a pillow. Ironically the only person who could not sleep on that occasion turned out not to be Daniel but rather Darius – the man who had the most comfortable and secure bed in the kingdom.

I am well aware that Jesus said that if we have faith in the size of a grain of mustard seed we can call upon a mountain to be removed and be cast into the sea. It is important to note though that, whilst that is obviously true, it often takes more faith to climb a mountain than it does to make it vanish. It takes the faith of Daniel that can rest on promises, the faith of Moses that can see the invisible, the faith of the Hebrew boys who could stand in the fire unsinged and clothed in divine asbestos, instead of prayer for the fire to go out. That's faith.

There are situations when faith has to see further than even the possible end of the trauma – even as far as eternity.

I once saw a film of an interview with Corrie Ten Boom. She was sitting in a garden doing some needlework as the interviewer put his questions to her. One of the things he asked was something like this, 'Corrie, tell us what it was like in that concentration camp. Did you ever fear that you would never get out. How did you cope?' Corrie explained the basis of her faith at that time. It was what she did next that I will never forget. She lifted the embroidery so that the camera could get a good shot of it. The side she showed was a tangled mess – a confusing pattern of coloured threads. She then turned it over to the other side. She had been embroidering words and they read, 'God is love'. Some things we understand now; other things are made clear later in life. Other matters still, will never be resolved in our minds until we get to the 'other side'.

Adoniram Judson was captured by ruthless natives in Burma. He was strung up by his thumbs, tortured and then thrown into a filthy prison cell. 'What now of your plans to convert the heathen?' his tormentors mocked. His answer must have astonished them, 'My future is as bright as the promises of God', he replied. Israel's spies had investigated the Promised land. Adoniram Judson was the citizen of a land of promises. He could probably see more from his vantage point of suffering than most of us ever see in our comparatively painless world.

I used to live in Cheltenham. Outside the town is a place called Birdlip Hill. The panoramic view that meets your eyes stretches for mile after mile. Mountain tops are made for visions – but not always. Isaiah spoke of a 'valley of vision'.[8] He understood that some people can see further when they are 'down' than when they were 'up'.

Speaking of the danger of shortsightedness in periods of suffering Paul writes to the church at Corinth, 'For our light and momentary troubles are achieving for us an eternal glory that far outweighs them all. So we fix our eyes not on what is seen but on what is unseen. For what is seen is temporary but what is unseen is eternal.'[9] The emphasis again is the focus of our vision, on the place on which we fix our eyes. God had once said to Abraham, 'Lift up your eyes from where you are'.[10] He often has to say it to us.

The problem is that there are none so blind as those that will not see. If the rich young ruler had done that then he would not have gone away sorrowful. His eyes were fixed on his possession. If jealous Diotrephes had done it then his local church would not have been so poorly off under his leadership and could have benefited from ministries other than his own. His eyes were fixed on position and personal status.[11]

Families need to guard against shortsightedness. Partners looking for fulfilment in their marriages need to look beyond themselves and consider the needs of their spouse. They will probably find fulfilment by default. As families too we need ever to be aware of the lonely, the alienated, the divorced.

The Bible says that, 'God puts the lonely in families.'[12] If He does then it is our families in which He is going to put them. There are no others that He has got. This does not mean that we have all to run out and live in community. It means that our doors, and our hearts, are not closed to those who need to know the warmth of our lives.

Churches need to guard against shortsightedness. The spiritual vision of any local congregation is usually revealed through its prayer meeting: not just in the numbers of those that attend but also in the spectrum of the petitions that it makes. Praying that concentrates only on 'us and ours', or even worse, on 'me and mine' needs badly to consult the Divine Oculist. Fellowships that have eyes that can focus on needs outside their own church and Denomiantion and see the broader issues of the Kingdom of God are vision churches. National issues that grieve the heart of God should grieve our hearts too. A church only has twenty-twenty vision when it can see things as God sees them. When Jeremiah's eyes ran down with rivers of tears it has been said that the tears were not only his own. God was weeping through him. When God weeps through us we will find ourselves crying out against issues such as the crime of abortion and when we have finished praying we will lobby, protest and demonstrate until such national sins are eliminated from the statute books and the streets.

The problem with good vision is that the more the Christian sees the more they feel responsible for. Only blinkered Believers can ever feel complacement; only those with tunnel vision can ever 'sit at ease with Zion'.

Churches that are free from spiritual shortsightedness will be those who are praying for those who are not yet Christians and will be making plans to reach them. Praying for, 'sinners to come in' is hardly what is called for. We call them sinners, and so they are. God sees them also as lonely, hurting, alienated and sometimes despised or oppressed. It is only when we begin to see them through His eyes we become near enough to touch them with His love.

Longsightedness

Obviously, this is the opposite optical problem to the one we have just considered. It occurs when people can see well at a distance but remain oblivious to things that are close at hand. The writer of the book of Proverbs says, 'A discerning man keeps wisdom in view but a fool's eyes wander to the ends of the earth.'[13] This eye disorder can be diagnosed in many areas of our Christian lives.

59

1. *Attitude to Service*

Some years ago a Bible College received an application from one of the Mission Fields operating within their Denomination. The missionary communicated to the Principal that they had a young man whom they considered to have a great deal of potential. They wished him to be trained in Britain and then later to return to his homeland to work there.

His application proved to be successful and on the first day of his college term was awakened by the ringing of an early morning bell. It was the custom in the college that each day before breakfast the students were to be engaged in manual work around the college complex. Chores such as painting, electrical installation, remedial work on the building or the digging of land drains would be typical.

When the bell rang the overseas students inquired of the two other young men who shared the room what the bell signified. When they told him his reaction was simply to turn over in his bed with the words, 'The prophet of the Lord does not dig ditches.' When the Head Boy came to see why the student was missing from his work detail he too was met with the same retort, 'The prophet of the Lord does not dig ditches.' No amount of explaining or counselling would help. He adamantly refused to be involved in any manual duties whatsoever on the grounds that he had received a great calling, and work of this nature was not part of it. A few weeks later he was to be seen walking down the long college driveway untrained, undisciplined and unrepentant. As he lugged two heavy suitcases into the distance he was still heard to mutter, 'The prophet of the Lord does not dig ditches.'

He was suffering from a chronic case of longsightedness. He had a vision of the distant future but was unable to recognise the simple steps that might lead in time to his ultimate destination becoming a reality. He had disqualified himself from spiritual service on the grounds of poor eyesight.

Unfortunately the symptoms cited in this case history are not isolated ones. There are many other Christians who could be diagnosed with the same disease: people who believe that God has got great plans for them but do little in the here and now. The affliction is found in those who pray that they might be used to win many for Christ but are a poor witness at home and rarely present a clear testimony verbally, or actively, in the place where they work. The old missionary adage remains eternally true, 'There is little use sending a lamp to China that will not burn at home.'

Some lamps that are willing to burn at home choose to keep their light in reserve for the big event. 'There is a big Evangelistic Outreach planned for May but now its only January – sixteen weeks away.' To the long-sighted disciples of his day Jesus said, 'Do you not say, 'Four months more and then the harvest'. I tell you *open your eyes* and look at the fields! They are ripe for harvest.'[14]

2. *Attitude to Giving*

At an ever increasing rate, glossy, expensively produced magazines calling for urgent financial assistance for their particular project tumble through our letter boxes. Some of these are very worthy causes and deserved to be supported, but sadly, some are less so. We have to doubt the wisdom of sending large amounts of money several thousand miles away when the work of the home church is in a state of neglect or the local leadership is forced to exist on a subsistence level. A great number of para-church organisations are the handmaiden of the local congregation and deserve every form of practical support. The solution is not to be found in either a shortsighted or long-sighted focus, it is discovered in a balanced and prayerfully planned vision for church, and personal budgeting.

3. *Attitude to Praying*

I adopted the practice in one of the churches that I pastored to invite various of our Lay Leaders to bring a brief message to the people at our weekly prayer meeting. We wanted to devote the majority of our time to getting down to prayer so the short message became to be known eventually as the 'ten minute word'. The content was usually of a faith building and encouraging nature and more than once proved to be the match that lit the fuse of some very profitable times of intercession. One of those meetings was to be very special indeed.

On this occasion I had asked the youngest of our deacons to speak. After an opening time of worship I read the requests and then handed the meeting over to him. He surprised us all by giving his talk the title, 'How to answer your own prayers'. One of the prayer requests we were to bring was for the Lord to provide regular transport for a group of disabled people who wanted to attend the church. Instead of praying, he asked for a show of hands to determine how many of the congregation passed the Centre for the Disabled on their way to church and had spare seats in their car. The next request was for a supply of much needed drugs for one of our Mission Fields. Instead of praying he suggested that the stewards take up an offering in the meeting – something that we did not normally do in a midweek service. By the time that he had finished we had hardly anything left to pray for. It was one of the best prayer meetings I have ever been in and taught us all the lesson that it was all too easy to have a long-sighted attitude when approaching God in prayer. I have since tried never to ask God to do tomorrow what I am perfectly capable of doing for myself, or someone else, today. The epistle of James puts it well:

> What good is it, my brothers, if a man claims to have faith but has no deeds? Can such faith save him? Suppose a brother or sister is without clothes and daily food. If one of you says to him, 'Go, I wish you well; keep warm and well fed, but does nothing about his physical needs, what good is it? In the same way, faith by itself, if it is not accompanied by action, is dead.[15]

4. *In our Perception of Spiritual Truth*

I continually meet people who are able to look a long way back to a place of personal failure but fail to see a God near at hand who is willing to forgive those who come to him in real and sincere repentance.

Others are similarly long-sighted but their point of focus is different. They forever hark back to a previous era when, 'God really did wonderful things'. For some reason it usually was a time when they personally were at their peak physically and spiritually. No one would deny anyone their recollections of the past. There is nothing inherently sinful about nostalgia. The problem with memory though is that it is often very selective. It tends to highlight the good times at the expense of the bad. It is hard to look at the past objectively. This is probably why the writer of the book of Ecclesiastes wrote, 'Do not say, 'Why were the old days better than these?' For it is not wise to ask such questions.'[16]

Longsightedness is often an optical malady that accompanies a certain type of Second Coming teaching. An over emphasis on the several kinds of end-time signs seems to lead some to emulate the ostrich and hide away from the decadence of a lost culture and, in the more acute cases, back off from evangelical as well as social action. It is assumed that because the world is going to be destroyed and judgement is inevitable that is probably best just to let the process take its course.

Ostrich heads are buried in sand and sand is found in deserts. It is only the lives of the arid and dry that would ever wish to drop out from the real world. Salt and light communities are made for penetration not for hibernation. God has not set His Church apart to be colonies of packet-dwellers and the inhabitants of bushels. The long-sighted who wish to live in such a way have effectively turned their doctrinal eschatology into an act of escapology.

A tourist once decided to take a holiday with a difference. Instead of the package tour he was used to he felt that this time he would hike through Switzerland; getting as far away as he possibly could from the normal tourist routes. One day he came across a beautiful mansion by a lake. Even more impressive than the magnificent architecture of the building was the breathtaking beauty of the gardens that surrounded it. Manicured lawns, flower-laden terraces, a riot of colour that cascaded down even as far as the water's edge. The strange things was that nobody seemed to be around. Eventually he came across the gardener.

'Excuse me sir', he said. 'Is this a private residence, a stately home or a health resort?'

'Oh, it's a private home all right, but no one lives here just now. My master is away on business a lot of the time and the place is only really occupied on a couple of occasions during the year.'

'But you keep the grounds in such an immaculate condition', observed the tourist. 'I suppose that you look after them just as if the owner could come home tomorrow.

'Not at all', replied the gardener. 'I care for it on the assumption that the master may come home today.'

Jesus is returning and the signs of His coming are left there for our benefit, but not to invoke in us a sense of smug complacency. His command is clear, 'Occupy until I come.'[17]

No fixed focus

A society that rejects the concept of absolutes will always have a problem with focus. If man is put at the centre of the universe a problem immediately emerges. Embracing an ever changing perspective on moral issues, his evolutionary concept of right and wrong hardly creates for him an immovable pole star by which he can chart its course. The womb of situation ethics rarely gives birth to secure offspring. Politics and secular systems of belief, for the same reason, have an inbuilt self destruct mechanism. Nothing can be trusted when mankind alone is at the helm.

Religion too, seen merely as a structure for man's search for God, cannot supply the answer. It was religious people that crucified Jesus – zealots convinced that they were accomplishing the will of God by doing so. So meticulous were they in their code of belief that they asked Pilate that the legs of those on the cross might be broken and the bodies removed in order that the Sabbath would not be desecrated.[18] The fact that they were crucifying the Messiah never entered their minds. They considered themselves to be living in the brightest aura of revealed truth. The reality was that they were spiritually blind. Any focus that they had was centred on the Law and the Prophets. They were unable to see as far as the fulfilment even though He was within their very grasp. Pilate, only hours earlier, had made the same mistake. Whilst asking Jesus the universal question, 'What is Truth?' he remained totally unaware that the subject of his question stood before him; the very object of his gaze.

Committed Christians declare themselves as having discovered the ultimate focus point of the universe in the person of Jesus. They proclaim their discovery with the enthusiasm of the writer to the Hebrews who says, 'Let us fix our eyes on Jesus, the author and perfector of our faith.'[19] Finding a focus is one thing: what we as Christians often find more difficult is retaining our gaze. A glance or even a long look is insufficient. The word 'fix' has a ring of permanence about it.

This was the problem Peter faced. While the other disciples as they looked across the water thought they had seen a ghost he recognised Jesus and was enthusiastic enough to leave his less adventurous friends in the boat and step out into the sea to go to Him. With eyes firmly fixed on Jesus he was well able to resist the gravitational pull that would have, naturally speaking, sucked any one of us under. Locked into Christ's navigational beam he felt he was well able to walk on water. However, when he checked the on-board computer of his mind the engine of his faith cut out. Christ-centred he was able to walk across the sea. Problem-centred he considered himself skating on thin ice. He trusted the wrong instrument panel and lost altitude almost immediately. He was sunk until he was saved – just like the rest of us.

The temptation to allow our eyes to wander from Christ to other things is ever present and comes in several forms.

1. *The Attraction of the Tangible*

It is said that Wesley one day was travelling with a man who, by his conversation, was exhibiting a great deal of spritual pride. The evangelist was having to suffer a long list of all that his companion had done for God and was being favoured with all the details of this man's deep and devotional life of prayer. Not being able to stand it any longer Wesley dismounted from his horse, and pointing at it, said to his boastful friend, 'I will gladly give you this horse if you can even pray for five minutes without taking your eyes off the one to whom you are speaking.' The arrangement was set. The man began to lift his voice to God but, before he had prayed for even two minutes, broke from his intercession to ask, 'Excuse me, does this deal include the saddle?'

The rich young ruler, a yuppie by some people's standard, set out to see Jesus and was willing to become a disciple. He was later to find out that he was carrying too much ballast to be really 'upwardly mobile'. Jesus was not in any way inferring that there was anything inherently evil about wealth or pure about poverty. What He was doing was giving him an eye examination. The simple test determined all to quickly his real point of focus. Here was yet another who was to be disqualified from spiritual service on the grounds of deficient eyesight. There would have been no difficulty in him possessing his possessions. The problem was that his possessions had possessed him.

2. *The Attraction of Popularity*

Pontius Pilate was staggered by Jesus. People who appeared before him with the threat of crucifixion hanging over their heads were not usually known for their poise. Jesus broke the cast iron sterotype that Pilate had always known. A typical scenario when the doors of his judgement hall were opened would be for the prisoner to drop before him begging, like a manacled maniac, for his life. Jesus was cool and in control. The Prince of Peace was living up to His Name – even there.

The interrogation over, Pilate presented Jesus to the people and told them that he could find no fault in him. Having given them the option of the release of either their Messiah or a convicted terrorist, he felt he was more than a little confident who their choice would be. Surely Jesus would live to see another day. He was to live to see eternity but that was no thanks to Pilate. The Gospel writers supply two reasons for his willingness to consign Jesus to be crucified. Firstly, He did not want anything to jeopardise his job – the people had made it plain that to release Jesus would imply that he was not Caesar's friend. Secondly, Mark records that he sent Christ to the cross because he wanted to 'satisfy the crowd'.[20]

I meet folk all the time who would like to be more involved in the life and witness of their fellowship but who stop short of their objective because of fear. Yet the fear is not a fear of God, it is most often a fear of what other people will think of them if they fail. They are the people who would like to pray publicly but feel that they cannot compete with the eloquence or theological precision of others – too easily forgetting that God is not interested in the breadth of our vocabulary but in the depth of our sincerity. They are the people who would like to witness more openly but are afraid that if they do so someone might ask them a question that they cannot answer. Every endeavour to progress further in their walk with God is accompanied with Peter's sinking feeling. And why? The focus is wrong. Eyes that hone in on our insufficiency, or the threat presented by other people, are looking in the wrong direction.

3. *The Attraction of Involvement*

A friend of mine who is a lecturer in Business Management suggested to me recently that there were four kinds of people in the world. Those who watch things happen, those to whom things happen, people who do not know what is happening, and people who make things happen. Most of us would like to think of ourselves as being in the final category – but at what cost?

Think of the time when Mary, sitting at the feet of Jesus, is conspicuously absent from the kitchen. Hold an interview with Martha and ask her what she is doing. She will probably say she was working for Jesus, yet He wanted her, as well as Mary, to be in communion with Him at that moment. Most of us have made the very same mistake at some time in our lives; involved in activity not initiated by God. Stop us in our tracks and, barely catching our breath to answer, we will convey how busy we are – on the Master's business. At such times we become very vulnerable to making Him meals He has not ordered. Even service becomes counter productive when it takes our eyes off Jesus.

Walking with our eyes open

Creative photographers tell us that the placing of a filter on the front of the camera lens can do wonders. An ultra violet or a polarising filter can keep the image true by coping with unusually bright light sources or dealing with the reflection of light upon water. Others are used for effect, to capture an image that is not really there. A tobacco coloured filter used on a grey day will give the final print a nostalgic sepia effect. A red filter can produce a sunset on the most ordinary of nights.

Reality can never be truly recorded when a filter is in place. To have truly open eyes we must live totally filter-free. If what we see in life is only understood 'in the light' of how our popularity or bank balance is affected then our spiritual vision will be perpetually marred. Jesus, said 'The eye is the lamp of the body. If your eyes are good, your whole body will be full of darkness. If then the light within you is darkness, how great is that darkness.'[21]

1. *Walking in single-mindedness*
The Apostle Paul was single minded. His eye was fixed so much on Christ that he was able to say, 'This one thing I do: forgetting what is behind and straining towards what is ahead, I press on toward the goal to win the prize for which God has called me heavenward in Christ Jesus.'[22]

Speaking at the funeral of Dawson Trotman, the founder of the Navigators, Billy Graham said, 'Here was a man who did not say, 'These forty things I dabble at,' but, 'This one thing I do.'

Naturalists tell us that one of the reasons that it is so difficult to catch a frog is that its vision is like a blackboard wiped clean. The only thing that it sees are those things that conern its survival. The mind is programmed to relegate other things out of sight. A person that can put a priority on the things that really matter, who can 'discriminate between things that differ', is someone who enjoys a good perspective on reality. Most of us have no problem with discerning between right and wrong. Our real problems usually lie in recognising the difference between the good and the best.

Single mindedness assumes direction and direction assumes a goal. Shortsighted Christians do not have a goal – they simply stumble on from day to day. Long-sighted people sometimes do have an objective but it is seldom realised because it has not been broken down in short term attainable steps. Vision must be married to a goal. Outlook always determines outcome.

One day a man, noticing a group of builders at work, asked them what it was they were making. The first man said, 'I'm making a wall, anyone can see that.' The second responded, 'I'm making five pounds an hour, but what's that got to do with you?' The third man replied, 'I'm creating a section of a church building that will stand one day to the glory of God.'

One man saw only bricks, another only money. The third was working with a nobler goal. It is not so much 'what' I am building, that is important to God. He is far more interested in the 'why'.

2. *Walking in a personal revelation*

The young people in a church that I once pastored arranged a sponsored event that involved going on a midnight hike across the Malvern hills. I was invited to go along with them, and I did.

When a fleet of minibuses dropped us at the location at which we were to commence our walk everyone was together in one group. Inevitably, because some are fitter, more enthusiastic, or even impatient, before too long some groups stretched ahead leaving others in their wake. Torch beams punctuated the dark air with narrow corridors of light and, with the groups now separated, the one from the other, by several yards, an aerial view of us must have looked for all the world like a string of shiny beads meandering snake-like along the dark countryside.

I soon discovered that this was going to be an ideal opportunity for me to catch up with some pastoral chats that I had wanted to make with a number of young folk and set my mind to spend a few minutes in each of the groups as we strolled along in the bracing but beautiful night air.

Having spent a little time with the young people at the rearmost group I noticed to my dismay that the batteries in my torch had suddenly lost power and within a second or two the light was completely extinguished. Throughout the hike while walking in other people's light there was no problem. The difficulty only arose when stumbling and tripping through the dark stretches between the groups. I was fortunate by the time morning came not to have scraped my shins and turned my ankles more seriously than I had.

What happened to me physically happens to people spiritually all the time. A person may read a book, listen to a tape or hear a message on a subject such as 'Seven Steps to Walking on Water'. It really has a great impression upon them to begin with. They feel that they have discovered a formula that will prove to be an elixir for all their ills. Sadly, in one dark night of the soul the remedy somehow fails to work. They had been trying to walk in another person's light.

Some principles of faith can, and should, be applied by those who have only recently come to know Christ. Other things evolve as the result of a process generated through experience. The process need not take a great deal of time. On many occasions I have witnessed recently converted folk, after only a few months, accelerating past trudging Christians who have been 'on the road' many years. It is depth of experience not length of experience that really matters with God.

Power Vision

When Solomon said, 'Without a vision the people

perish,'[23] he was making a statement that would be drawn upon by almost everyone who would ever address the subject of spiritual revelation. I often think of the verse when leaving my house on a wintery morning and watching motorists with frozen windscreens steering their mobile igloos through the streets and peering through the small area that has been scraped free of the offending ice.

It is the positive side of the argument that is really exciting: an understanding of the things that really matter is the road to perfect sight. It can only adequately be described as 'Power Vision'. It is the realm in which Knowledge really is Power.

'If only I had known . . .' I wonder how many times that is said within an average lifetime. The implication is of course that, had we known, we would have done things differently. It can apply to the purchase of an unreliable car, choosing an unsatisfactory venue for a holiday or entering a career that proves, in retrospect, to be something less than fulfilling. This though is only half the story for, as every Christian knows, it also refers to things we wished we had done – or at least done earlier. For those who came to Christ in later life, Salvation is a case in point.

Francis Bacon is the one to whom the quotation is credited when in his work, *Christian Meditations* he wrote, 'Knowledge itself is Power'. Though he may have coined the phrase at the turn of the sixteenth century, the truth itself transcends time.

Knowing God spells Power
When the Apostle Paul confessed to the church at Philippi that he counted everything a loss compared to the supassing greatness of knowing Christ and then went on to say that his greatest ambition was, 'To know

Christ and the power of His resurrection . . .'[24] we rarely make the link between 'knowledge' and 'power' in this vital statement. Knowing Christ is the prerequisite of experiencing His power and it is through that knowledge that the power flows. It is no coincidence that the One who knows most in the universe is also the most powerful. Omniscience is married to omnipotence. Similarly, it is the Believer who is the most sensitive to the heart and mind of God that becomes the vessel He most often uses to transmit His power and His might. 'The people who know their God – shall do exploits.'[24] Well might P T Forsyth write, 'You must live with people to know their problems and live with God to solve them.'

If a man or woman knows anything at all about God, the first thing they discover is that they can trust Him. As this 'knowledge' is in the area of faith it needs to be pointed out that the knowing is of the heart and not the head. To 'know' God with the head would imply that we can understand Him and no finite mind can ever understand Him whose ways are 'past finding out'. The Christian lives not in information but in revelation. There is a sense, in the spiritual realm at least, that is not just a case of what you know but of Who you know.

Knowledge of God really is power. When Job said that he knew that his Redeemer was alive he had power over his suffering. When the Psalmist wrote under Divine inspiration, 'Be still and know that I am God' he declared to generations in every era that it was possible to have power over anxiety and emotional trauma. By declaring as Paul did that, 'We know that in all things God works for the good of those who love Him, who have been called according to His purpose' he revealed the possibility of power over fear of the future. And, just in case anyone was in any doubt that power through

74

knowledge only affected the temporal and not the eternal he stressed to the younger Timothy, 'I know whom I have believed and am convinced that He is able to guard what I have entrusted to Him for that day'.[25] Someone has said that there are three classes of people in the world. Those who are afraid, those who do not know enough to be afraid, and those who know their Bible. Power vision reveals truth that really does set you free.

Knowing the Enemy spells Power
Nobody who can remember anything about the *Spycatcher* trials could ever doubt it. All the resources of the British Government were marshalled against the publication of a book. And for what? So that no information can be released that may be of value to an alien power.

Is there a spiritual equivalent of the Official Secrets Act? There most certainly is not! The Scripture makes it absolutely clear that, as far as the works of the Enemy are concerned, 'We are not ignorant of his devices.' Another translation has, 'In order that Satan might not outwit us. For we are not unaware of his schemes.'[26] In other words, 'We know what he is up to'. We know that he will sometimes try to masquerade as an angel of light. It comes as no surprise. Jesus has won the victory over him and His victory has become our victory. A roaring lion he may be but a toothless lion for all that. Carlos Ortiz tells in his book *Cry of the human heart* how on one occasion Smith Wigglesworth was awakened by something in his room one night. Lighting a candle he saw Lucifer at the end of his bed. 'Oh, it's only you', said Wigglesworth – blew out the candle, turned over on his side and went back to sleep.

Because we know his wiles so well the Christian has

no excuse for sinning. We can no longer say that we are 'only human'. God's spirit dwells within us and we have the mind of Christ. If we sin we choose to sin. There is not a Born Again Believer anywhere who has ever been tricked into sinning. Knowledge of the Enemy is Power Vision.

Knowing Ourself spells power

Every town or city has its 'bagmen' – tramps that wander the streets carrying with them, usually in an assortment of plastic bags, virtually all that they own. Often the contents of empty bottles, blankets and ragged clothes are a true reflection of their material wealth. Sometimes it is not. In a town where I once lived was a man who walked the streets in such a way. He was dishevelled, ragged and rich. He could have worn the best suits in town, eaten well and have afforded to live in a fashionable area. Instead, because of his state of mind he lived a life of material destitution. He did not realise who he was.

Though the Christian may not find it too difficult to sing the contemporary song *Jehovah Jireh my Provider* or the older hymn, *He is all I need* it is sometimes something less than easy to live in the experience of the truth. Perhaps far too many of us live like spiritual bagmen from day to day when our Father has promised to supply all our needs according to his riches in Christ Jesus. Though people who have a spirit of poverty are quick to point out the qualifications – 'He has only promised to supply our *needs*' That is not the qualification at all! He has promised to supply our needs, 'According to His glorious riches in Christ Jesus'[27] – that meets my needs and far more beside. God is a great Giver. As a son I should not only be expected to give cheerfully but also to consider myself a willing beneficiary of His generosity. God never gives to the greedy. He gives, spiritually and materially, not that we may be reservoirs but that we might be tributaries through which His grace can flow to others.

It is said that twenty years before the Gold Rush descended upon the Klondike that a poor farmer and his family watched helplessly as the bills piled up on their kitchen table. What was he using as a paperweight to keep his debts in place? You've guessed it. A shiny old rock that he had found weeks before lying by a river bed – a lump of gold. It says in Obadiah that the house of Jacob will 'possess its possessions'.[28] Perhaps we should too. Hosea spoke of those who were destroyed for lack of knowledge. Knowing who we are, and what we have, is power over spiritual and material poverty.

There are those who would argue that power is only really attained through strength and material wealth. I think I'll go along with Jeremiah, who records:

Let not the wise man boast in his wisdom or the strong man boast of his strength or the rich man boast of his riches, but let him who boasts boast about this: that he understands and knows me, that I am the Lord who exercises kindness, justice and righteousness on earth, for in these I delight, declares the Lord.[29]

When Vision Dims

In the normal course of events eye sight diminishes with advancing years. Spiritual eye sight needs not be so affected. On the contrary, there is no reason why it should not be enhanced by the passing of time.

As we have seen, every optical malady that we have investigated has been the product of a spiritual disease. When Jesus gave the Pharisees an eye examination He discovered that in some cases their blindness was caused by the presence of a foreign object in their eyes. He saw some attempting to remove specks of sawdust out of the eyes of others when they had long beams of wood sticking out of their own. A bizarre picture by any standards; protruding planks are not conducive to clear vision. Jesus made it clear that before anyone takes it upon himself to be an optician he needs to first cast his eyes upon himself.

Vision is not just for the use of seeing where I am going. It is for seeing where I am. In biblical times the torch used on a dark night differed greatly from the instruments that we use today. No multi-function Ever-Ready beam shedding its light solely on the path ahead! The burning torches used in those days shone as much on the user as it did on to the path. Seeing 'where I am' before God has a priority over seeing 'where I am going' before the world. The Psalmist noted the order of precedence when he wrote, 'Your word is a lamp to my feet and a light to my path'.[30]

When John experienced that remarkable vision on the isle of Patmos he was permitted to see unfolded a message to which we now refer to as the 'Seven churches of Revelation'. One of those churches was situated in Laodicea. This city boasted a profitable clothing industry, banks and a medical instituation. Pointing at a parallel to their conditions as Christians God says, 'You do not realise that you are wretched, pitiful, poor, blind and naked'.[31] There was, however, a prescription that contained an antidote to their malaise, 'Buy from me salve that you can put on your eyes, so you can see.' The purchase though can be so costly that it is a price that some are not willing to pay.

When Naaman knocked the door of the prophet's house he anticipated red carpet treatment. He was after all Commander in Chief of the army of Aram. He was in for a shock. When the leprous leader learned that Elisha did not feel it necessary to even come to the door to speak with him – but sent his servant instead, he was filled with chagrin. The messenger who came did not endear himself to him and the message was even less palatable. Turning on his heels, after being told to wash in the Jordan seven times, he retorted, 'I thought that he would surely come out to me and stand and call on the name of the Lord his God, wave his hand over the spot and cure me of my leprosy. Are not Abana and Pharpar, the rivers of Damascus, better than any of the waters of Israel?'[32] Naaman was thinking of a hidden cost that would be apparent at that moment only to him.

No one would believe that a man who had distinguished himself on the field, and had to face the scenes of mutilation that were a part of every warring landscape, was now frightened of a little dirty water in the Jordan river. There had to be another reason, and there was.

Naaman would not have been able to remember the time when his parents gave him his name, a name that, though sounding foreign to us, would have been understood by admiring family and friends for what it meant – pleasant and beautiful. His meteoric rise to fame would have given every indication that his name had been an excellent omen for him. That was of course until the disease was discovered. A small white skin blemish to begin with. Nothing that would cause too much concern. Later the whole dreadful truth was revealed. The diagnosis was leprosy. The prognosis was death.

Most lepers lost not only their health. In the wake of such a tragedy, there usually followed loss of friends and self esteem. Self esteem was all he had to hang on to. Self esteem reflected in the magnificence of his apparel that left as little as possible of his diseased frame on view. This was why the prophet's apparent rebuff had affected him so badly. The remedy was surely too expensive – even for him. Had he had not shame enough already. There was no second opinion to consult. He decided to pay the price.

He inched his way down to the river and began slowly to remove all the outward trappings of his status and his success. Bit by bit every trace of the insignia of his importance was stripped away until there by the river bank he stood – in full view of even the most lowly foot soldier. Stripped to the waist. There was no chance of a quick dip to get it over with. Elisha's prescription had been precise – seven times. He paid the price with the currency of his pride and discovered that humility is still legal tender with God. His condition was transformed. He became as beautiful as his name had declared him to be.

Leprosy is often used in the Scriptures as an analogy of sin as cleansing is a sign of repentance. It is a costly remedy but it is the only one that will do.

Oswald Chambers has spoken of repentance thus:

> The essence of repentance is that it destroys the lust of self-vindication; wherever that lust resides the reptentance is not true. Repentance brings us to the place where we are willing to receive any punishment under heaven so long as the law we have broken is justified . . . The judgements of God leave scars and the scars remain until I humbly and joyfully recognise that the judgements are deserved . . . Holiness is based upon repentance and the holy man is the most humble man you meet. My realisation of God can be measured by my humility.[33]

When lubricating tear ducts fail to do their work and the eyes become dry, eye sight is certain to be affected. Dry eyes and hard hearts often reside in the same body. We too often think of repentance as being something that occurs at salvation. Seldom do we realise that the Lord requires that we live in a spirit of repentance in our daily walk with Him. When we first come to Christ repentance means doing a 'U turn'. Backsliding Christians often have to return to the place where they first 'lost their way' before they can have the vision that they once had of God, restored.

My grandfather spent much of his ministry in pioneering churches. On one occasion he was invited to speak at a Convention in one of the churches that he launched years earlier. Whilst speaking he happened to say in his message in reference to repentance, 'You will find God where you left him'. Out of the corner of his eye he noticed a man get up and quietly leave the church. The meeting over, he noticed the man had returned and who on doing so related to him the following story. It turned out that this man had been converted in the original Evangelisitc Crusade from which the church had been formed years earlier. He spoke of how his life had been radically changed and transformed. Then, several months later, he had been walking in the centre of the town and noticed his little daughter on the other side of the street. When their eyes met she ran out, without looking, into the middle of the road to meet her father. She was hit by a passing lorry and was killed instantly. The man related how he had stood by the side of the road that day and cursed the God that would take his only child from him. Never again would he darken the door of a church and from that moment bitterness, like a cancer, took root within his life.

He had come to that Convention meeting that evening

only out of curiosity to see the visiting Evangelist. Where had he gone during the service? Cued by the comment, 'You will find God where you left Him', he had gone to the very spot in the road where he had cursed God those years earlier. He had looked up to God and with tears rolling down his cheeks had asked for forgiveness. The bitterness was uprooted, his soul was filled with the peace, contentment and joy that had been absent for so long. He could see again. His vision had been restored. His eyes had been washed with tears. The eye salve had been purchased but was worth every penny. Some people will give anything for their sight.

5: Open Heart

Biologically, the 350g of muscle that pumps about five litres of blood around the body of the average adult male makes the heart the most vital organ that we possess.

Biblically it has come to represent the centre of our entire mental and moral activity. It is seen as the source of all that is both rational and emotional. The heart is considered the seat of intellectual and spiritual life. It denotes the inner self as opposed to the external appearance. Solomon suggested that it should be securely guarded as it was the 'wellspring of life'.[1]

Jeremiah pointed out that it could never be trusted. He declared that it was, 'Deceitful above all things', beyond cure and even understanding. In the very first usage of the word in Scripture God describes mankind in Noah's day as those whose, 'Inclination and thoughts of their heart were evil all the time'. In New Testament times Jesus is recorded as saying, 'The things that come out of the mouth come out of the heart and these make a man unclean. For out of the heart come evil thoughts, murder, adultery, sexual immorality, theft, false testimony, slander.'[2] Hardly an impressive test report for that which constitutes the very core of man's nature – the root of his personality, the life-source of a soul yet to be regenerated. Were we to doubt the downward bias of the heart then the Bible will provide us with a thousand case histories and, if such evidence should not suffice, the history of our civilisation would supply us with a million more. A typical example of the fickleness of the human heart is portrayed in the account of Paul's shipwreck. Having found the safe sanctuary of land, a viper rose from the flames by which the prisoners warmed themselves and wrapped itself around the Apostle's arm. The inhabitants of the island immediately jumped to the conclusion that this man must be so villainous that as the sea had not taken its prey then the poisonous vengeance of a serpent's fangs would. But when they realised that he was not about to die they came to the decision that a god had come among them. The Lord Jesus encountered such fickleness in reverse. One day worshipped as the Son of God and given a palm-leaf path on which to enter Jerusalem He was, on another that would shortly follow, to witness the raucous din that cried out venomously for His crucifixion. So much for the human heart.

Counsel for the defence will challenge our argument on the grounds of society's evolutionary growth and maturity. 'That was two thousand years ago in an uncivilised world: this is the twentieth century.' Let them tell it to six million Jews slaughtered at the hands of a nation in Europe which could boast at the time of being in the vanguard of culture, education and technology.

To the National Commission of Nuclear Scientists in May 1946 Albert Einstein said, 'The release of atom power has changed everything except our way of thinking, and thus we are being driven unarmed towards a catastrophe . . . The solution of this problem lies in the heart of humankind.' With the track record that the human heart has got, few people will be holding their breath.

Thomas Ward Beecher is said to have put a card under a clock which continually ran slow on which were written the words, 'Don't blame my hands, the trouble lies deeper.' It would seem that, as ever, the heart of the human problem is the problem of the human heart.

For the Believer, both an Abdication and a Coronation has taken place in the heart. Self has been dethroned from the central precinct of power and in its place a new Sovereign has been crowned. Jesus has become Lord. It was not a bloodless coup, nor really a coup at all. Remarkably and uniquely the blood is shed by the Conqueror and not by the vanquished.

The problem is that a 'fifth column' remains within the heart conducting a guerrila warfare; inciting the flesh to rebellion. Sin – the factory that makes sins – has been blitzed and brought to the ground yet there is still a mopping up action to be employed. 'Self' has indeed been put to death yet, paradoxically, must still die daily.

To be able to effectively administer, the new occupying force in the person of the Holy Spirit, must be granted total jurisdiction within the new territory. If the heart, the seat of so much previous rebellion, is to be kept clear of any enemy incursion the foe must be allowed no foothold. There can be no landing strip of inconsistency in the life from which the enemy can launch an attack.

The Holy Spirit will also need to be permitted complete access to reconnoitre every corner of its domain. There can be no 'No Go' areas. Barricades cannot be countenanced. If Lordship is to be a reality the heart must remain totally open.

Open to the Light

King David was an open hearted man. 'Test me O Lord and try me', he would pray. 'Examine my heart and my mind.' In one of his psalms he summons the strongest of searchlights when he says, 'Search me O God, and know my heart; test me and know my anxious thoughts. See if there is any offensive way in me, and lead me in the way everlasting'.[3]

He was not submitting his life to an examination in the way that we might offer a suitcase to a customs official at an airport as if saying, 'I've told you I am clean, and if you want to you can check.' He was asking the Lord to look for David's own benefit – the way one might go to a specialist for a medical examination. 'Lord', he says, 'I wonder if you would take a look at my anxious thoughts and tell me what you think'. God already knows the secrets of the heart[4] but it is we who must allow them to be brought to the light in order that He might be able to do something about our condition. Nothing is as accurate as the cardiograph that the Great Physician takes. In Acts 1:24 and Acts 15:8 where it speaks of God 'knowing the heart' the Greek word *Kardiognostes* is actually used.

Prophets do not necessarily make good heart specialists. Take Samuel for example. God had told him that he was to visit Jesse for from amongst his sons would come one who would be king of Israel. One by one they came before him; Eliab, Abinadab, Shammah and the rest. Each one looked the part – tall, strong, muscular and macho. Samuel felt sure that one of these would be the right candidate. Samuel looked at them from the perspective of an MGM casting agent. God was looking for a man 'after His own heart'. Eliab would have been Samuel's first choice but, like a senior surgeon speaking to a junior doctor who had just made a wrong diagnosis God reprimanded him by saying, 'Do not consider his appearance or his height, for I have rejected him. The Lord does not look at the things man looks at. Man looks at the outward appearance, but the

Lord looks at the heart.'[5] Eventually David was called, chosen and anointed.

Nearly twelve hundred years later three men approached Jesus to offer themselves as disciples. None of them got the job. They had let themselves down at the interview. The first had proved impulsive. The second was clearly a procrastinator and the third was similarly insincere. Any discipleship agency would have passed them with flying colours. Their words could not be faulted and perhaps even their 'non-verbal communication', did not give them away. They failed because the Master's vision delved deeper. The Word was able to read them. If they had been around a few years later they would be able to hear for themselves that, 'The Word of God is living and active. Sharper than any double-edged sword, it penetrates even to the dividing soul and spirit, joints and marrow; it judges the thoughts and attitudes of the heart. Nothing in all creation is hidden from God's sight. Everything is uncovered and laid bare before the eyes of Him to whom we must give account.'[6]

It is said that only the surface of the sea is penetrated by light. Further down is half lit and in the deepest part there is absolute darkness. At 170 metres it can be as bright as a moonlight night. Light can only penetrate to a depth of 400 metres yet animal life exists 4,000 metres deep. Although after 400 metres all animals are blind, nothing escapes the gaze of God. He notices not only every sparrow that falls but every fish that sinks. David said, 'Surely you desire truth in the inner parts; you teach me wisdom in the inmost place.'

The personnel department of many major corporations demand that a successful interview should be followed by a medical examination. The heart will always be the prime subject for scrutiny before it can be established that we are 'fit to work'. Spiritual service requires no lesser standard, 'Who may ascend the hill of the Lord and who may stand in His holy place', asks David. The rhetorical question is answered with the words, 'He who has clean hands and a pure heart, who does not lift up his soul unto an idol or swear what is false'.[7] It is evident that God's stethoscopic inspection investigates two vital areas of the heart, listening for the murmurs of two destructive forces.

(a) *Hidden Idols*

One day the Elders of Israel came and sat down in front of Ezekiel. No doubt they looked an impressive bunch. It is likely that their status-conscious deportment would have put the fear of death in any lesser mortal. Ezekiel was not impresed. God had given him a 'Word of Knowledge' for, as they sat and stared at him the Lord said, 'Son of Man, these men have set up idols in their hearts'. As the Lord gave Ezekiel X-Ray eyes, He also handed him a pin to prick the balloon of their pomposity. It was a sad scene. Because they were leaders, they had not only developed a coronary complaint, they had done something far worse: they had put stumbling blocks in the way of the people they were leading. Things had got so bad that the Lord had to tell Ezekiel that even if He sent a world beating ministry team comprising of Noah, Daniel and Job it was still too late for the situation to be ministered into. The heart complaint was to prove fatal for far more people than the Elders themselves.[8]

When Lot's wife ran from Sodom to escape the sulphurous flames of God's judgement upon the city, she looked back. Her husband had been an important man. She had shared something of the status that went with his prestigious position but now, together with her possessions, it had all gone up in flames. She may have left Sodom geographically but Sodom, together with her idols, was still in her heart.

Goethe said, 'We are shaped and fashioned by what we love.' The Lord Jesus put it far more precisely when he told us that where our treasure is, there will our heart be also. The Psalmist prayed that the Lord would give him an 'undivided heart'. He knew, as you and I need to know, that as the idle are not willing to be used, the idolater cannot be used.

(b) *Impure Motives*

Sadly, it would seem that it is cynicism, rather than sincerity, that is rapidly becoming a hallmark of today's increasing secular society. The Church, God's alternative community, must, of all people, have a clean heart in this respect if it is to act as salt and light in the world in which it has been placed.

It is suggested that the Greek word for sincerity, *Eilikrineia*, may be derived from two words which together mean, 'judged in the sunlight'.[9]

Imagine if you will, going to a sculptor to order one of the status symbols that could be acquired in Bible days. What you are looking for is a 'head and shoulders' representation of either yourself or a member of your family, fashioned in stone. The order made and the deposit paid you wait for the day when the masterpiece is ready for collection. In the dimness of the sculptor's storeroom everything looks in order. The bust is taken away and in no time at all finds its way to a prominently placed plinth in your lounge awaiting the admiring glances of every guest who will enter your home.

What you are not aware of, is that when putting a final finishing touch to the aquiline nose of his handiwork, the tired sculptor's chisel slips. The nose is no more and lies amongst the discarded chippings at his feet. He has a choice. He can either start again from scratch or take the option that he eventually decides upon-fix the missing piece with wax. It was a common trick of the trade but the problem was that all too often in the heat of the home, perhaps in the midst of an important dinner party just as the new acquisition is the centre of the attention, the wax melts and the nose drops. You have literally 'lost face'. Due to this known practice most folk, before ever leaving the sculptor's studio, would take his handiwork to the window and judge it in the sunlight to see if both the art and the artist were sincere.

The Lord searches the heart for sincerity, reality and purity of motive. When the Lord tests our works the Bible says that it will be shown for what it is because the 'Day will bring it to light. It will be revealed with fire, and the fire will test the quality of each man's work.'[9] What we really are before God can only be effectively discerned inside the furnace of fire and the pressure of heat. Note that the emphasis of the verse is not on quantity but on quality. Two people may have been Christians for exactly the same amount of time, worshipped, witnessed and even tithed to the same degree yet their rewards could differ dramatically. If activity was generated by ambition, self-glory or an inordinate need to be fulfilled then the reward will be commensurate with the motivation. If our eyes are fixed on the wrong goal then our perspective will lose its sense of objectivity. There were four factors that motivated the Apostle Paul and he shares them with the church at Corinth during one of his letters to them. The first was the fear of the Lord. The second was the love of the Lord. The third was the need of the world and the fourth was the urgency of the hour.[10]

Charles Spurgeon wrote in his book *Lectures to My Students*, 'When a guitarist plays a chord and finds the instrument out of tune he stays his hand.' If the Believer is to be used by God, the heart must be clear of idols and clean in motive.

Open to Serve

The first convert in Europe was a woman. Lydia was a career woman, a female executive who dealt in high fashion. Of her conversion the Scripture records, 'The Lord opened her heart to respond to Paul's message.'[11] Having come to Christ her spontaneous reflex was one of service and she offers the Evangelistic team hospitality. Her open heart was immediately followed by an open home.

This seemed to have been Paul's experience too. In the account of his conversion in Acts 22 we find that his first question was, 'Who are you Lord?' and the second question was, 'What shall I do Lord?' The Lord immediately put him under delegated authority and he was told to seek out someone who would tell him. He was not to expect thunderous tones from on high every time the Lord wished to communicate with him. Hearing God through other people was not to be considered second class post. The authority that Lydia was to come under and the authority that Saul of Tarsus submitted to was the same authority that Jesus accepted in His Earthly ministry when he said, 'My Father works and I work.' If only we as Christians were always able to get that order of precedence correct. Again He says, 'I do nothing on my own but speak just what the Father has taught me.'[12]

Serving God is far less a difficulty than serving one another. Any of the disciples would have been willing to wash the feet of Jesus. It was when they were challenged to wash one another's feet that they were faced with a problem. Foot washing was the job of the lowliest servant in the household and because of that, service automatically took on the connotation of being somehow 'less than'. Jesus was to teach them that the one who wished to be great in the kingdom of heaven was to be the servant of all. The way up was the way down. Few folk have a problem with serving as the conductor of an orchestra, or even first violinist, but 'It takes more grace than tongue can tell to play the second fiddle well.'

Richard Foster has put it this way:

> Whenever there is trouble over who is the greatest there is trouble over who is the least. Most of us know that we will never be the greatest; just don't let us be the least. Radical denial gives the feeling of adventure. If we forsake all we have the chance of glorious martyrdom but in service we are banished to the mundane the ordinary and the trivial . . . Jesus does not reverse the pecking order, He abolishes it. [13]

There are three fundmantal symbols of servanthood.

a) *Obedience*

The first thing a Christian ever discovers about obedience is that it is not easy. It was not easy even for Jesus. The writer to the Hebrews enlightens us to the fact that Jesus, 'Although he was a son, he learned obedience from what he suffered and once made perfect, he became the source of eternal salvation for all who obey him . . .' Temptation was by no means a walkover for the Lord Himself and the same writer tells us why, 'Because He Himself suffered when He was tempted, He is able to help those who are being tempted.'[14] The 'perfection' to which the Scripture says Jesus attained was not a moral perfection – for He descended to earth and ascended to heaven in total unspoilt purity. It refers to a completeness that can only be accessed through experience. The Ivory Palaces would have been an Ivory Tower had Jesus not entered into our world, felt our pain, and encountered our weaknesses. As it is, He has and has become a High Priest who is 'touched with the feelings of our infirmities.'

Like most things that are worthwhile obedience exacts a price. It calls for submission at any cost. It will not act deferentially to comfort or convenience. It knows no compromise. Partial obedience is a contradiction in terms. There are times when God can call us to a particular sphere of service and, not willing to rise to the challenge, we ask to be obedient somewhere else. Lottie Moon found herself the only missionary in China at one part of the nineteenth century. She wrote, 'It seems queer that God would call five hundred preachers for Virginia alone and leave one lone woman for the whole of China.'

Obedience calls us to go beyond the emotional experience of the encounter with God into the step-by-step walk of radical discipleship. Too often we are willing to be reservoirs when God calls us to be tributaries. All too frequently we are tempted to stop short of God's destination for us because of the pull of self interest. This occurs when we build shrines at the altar of 'experience' and where the fact of the message becomes more important than the challenge of its content. It is a lot easier to sing hymns and choruses on the theme of spiritual warfare than it is to distinguish oneself on the field of battle.

Walking through the centre of Edinburgh a tourist or visitor could well be startled by the sound of canon fire. Those who know the city well would not be likely to even bat an eyelid. They would know that the source of the sound is the gun which fires each day, at 1 pm precisely, from the majestic castle that sits high in its grounds overlooking Princes Street. This canon, like the one in the *1812 Overture*, is a threat to no one as it is only firing for effect.

The Devil does not dive for cover when we sing if our battle cries are only words and are not to be followed by obedient kingdom service. Why should he tremble if he is in no danger of being scarred from our shrapnel?

If Moses had built a shrine at the burning bush where would the children of Israel have been today? If Paul had erected an altar on the Damascus road what would have become of the Christian church? The truth is that the slaves would have been emancipated and the Church would have been built. But not by Moses and not by Paul. God would have found those who were willing to make the full journey from encounter to obedience. The question put to Isaiah when he experienced a dramatic vision from heaven was not 'Are you enjoying yourself?', but, 'Whom shall I send?'[15]

Peter wanted to build a booth on the Mount of Transfiguration. Jesus was more interested in the plight of the demon possessed boy at the foot of the mountain than he was in creating a tourist attraction. The destinations of pilgrims is service, not shrines.

b) *Willingness*

It is quite possible to be submissive to God in a legalistic sense alone. This may be clinically defined as obedience but is not the obedience of the Open Heart.

I heard a story a few years ago of a little boy who was

94

taken to church but from his vantage point was unable to see what was going on at the front. He came to the conclusion that the only thing that he could do was to stand on his seat during the service. This solved his problem but it created several more for the folk who were sitting behind him, and not least for his mother who was most embarrassed by what he was doing. She asked her son gently to resume his seat but, looking down at her with defiant eyes, said with a fierceness that belied his three years of age, 'No I won't!'. Repeatedly he was asked and each request was met with the same rebuff. As a last resort his mother, not wanting the service to be disturbed any further suggested to him that if he refused to be obedient he was going to be in a great deal of trouble when he got home. This seemed to do the trick and the child sank sulkily down into his seat. After a few moments a little voice was heard to say, 'Mum?'

'What is it now', his mother retorted.

'I just want you to know,' he said, 'that I may be sitting down on the outside, but I'm standing up on the inside!'

I wonder how often my obedience has been a little like that. When I have been obedient to the will of God but it has not been really, 'from the heart'.[16]

It is said that Rees Howells would walk two miles each way to minister after working a twelve hour day at the mine. When one night he came from a meeting soaking wet and tired his father said to him, 'Son, I wouldn't do that for twenty pounds.' 'Neither would I for twenty pounds', came Rees Howells' reply.

This was no legalistic service. He was, as the Authorised Version of the Bible translates Psalm 110:3 'willing in the day of God's power' or, as the NIV translation has it, one of the troops who would be, 'willing on the day of battle'.

c) *Availability*

I have no idea to what degree the film *A Bridge Too Far* is an accurate account of the defence of the Bridge at Arnhem but when I saw it my mind was captured by the contrast that is made between two very different houses. The first is a house that overlooks the bridge. It is occupied by an elderly lady and her adult son. It is requisitioned by the army because its second floor provided an ideal vantage point for a machine gun placement due to its proximity to the bridge. The family of two find it necessary to move to a part of house that is relatively secure but in the midst of the mayhem of battle the son is sent by his mother to the commanding officer with the words, 'Mother says would you please try and keep the noise down.' It creates a humorous interlude and the officer is quick to remind the man that many lives are at risk and that there was a war going on.

The second house, more a stately home, lies some distance from the bridge. The casualties have been high and the wounded are in desperate need of attention. The senior officer rehearses as he walks up the long drive to the front door how he will tell the owner that he will need to commandeer their residence for the treatment of the dying. The door opened by the lady of the house, he begins his speech to the accompaniment of the sounds of battle in the distance. The lady interrupts him, 'This is no time for talking, bring them in immediately.' Within moments the house becomes a hospital. No thought for the dirt on the walls or the blood on the carpets. The wide and winding staircase lined with portraits done in oils is lined lower with the bodies of soldiers smeared with grease. An abiding memory of the film is of the owner in the midst of her invaded privacy holding the head of a dying soldier as she comforts him with the reading of the ninety-first psalm. What a contrast. And what a parallel with those who own the name of Christ yet concern themselves solely with the trivia and peripheral things of church life when there is a war going on; and while other serving saints involve themselves in the reality of the battle, often at great personal cost.

In the account of the entry of Jesus to Jerusalem there is a character who deserves far more attention from preachers than he receives: the owner of the donkey. For Jesus to ask his disciples to go down the street and untie a colt that would be found there is tantamount today to asking someone to go down a road and look for a car with the keys in the ignition and drive it off. There is little wonder that the disciples asked. 'What shall we do if someone tries to stop us?' To run, would have been one understandable option.

Jesus told them, in the event of them being challenged, to simply say, 'The Lord needs it.' Jesus was no more likely to steal a donkey than he was to take a car so we can assume that the man had previously put this animal at the Master's disposal. This is more than speculation for the identification of Christ as Lord to the owner clearly indicates that there was a commitment relationship in operation. I often wonder who the man was. He may well have been someone whom Jesus had healed or to whose home Christ had brought blessing. At some point he must have said something to the effect, 'If there is anything I can do for you – just let me know.' I wonder how many times we have all said something of that nature to the Lord. The fact is that if we have ever given him the title 'Lord' in our worship or our praying we have assumed His total sovereignty over our lives and our possessions. Jesus never requisitions anything against our will, so the man must have previously made the promise.

Making a commitment is not too difficult. It is when Jesus comes to our door and asks that we release to him that which has previously offered that problems sometimes arise. Few of us today have fettered donkeys. Our complaint is that we would serve more if our time was not tied up. We would give more if our money was not tied up, and we would witness more if we did not have the difficulty of being so tongue-tied.

Jesus saw no need to ask the man a second time for that which had been promised once. He assumes that if the Father is expected to stand by His word by His children; should not the sons too be willing to abide by the same family rule?

It comes as a surprise to some to learn that the Lord needs anything at all. How can he who, 'owns the cattle on a thousand hills' require, let alone need, anything from me?

The fact is that when we release into service that which, in title, is already his it is not He who is enriched. Instead, we are.

When the boy set off with his loaves and fishes to listen to Jesus perhaps the biggest miracle of all is that he did not eat them all before he got there. As he joined the vast crowd there was no way he could be aware either of the conversation that was going on between Jesus and His disciples or the fact that he was about to be enshrined for ever in the pages of biblical history.

When the disciples related to Jesus the problem he told them to provide food for the people themselves. The reply would have seemed cruel were there not a clear principle behind it. Jesus always brings us to the place where we acknowledge our powerlessness before we can experience His sufficiency. The Master then asked them to find out if there was anyone who had food with them. Andrew discovered the boy and found that he was willing to release his lunch, even to a perfect stranger – because the Lord needed it. But did the Lord really need it? In one sense, he did not. Even the Devil knew that. When Jesus entered into the desert to fast, prior to the commencement of His ministry, Satan had tempted Him to make bread out of stones.

Not only did Jesus not need fish sandwiches as the raw material for a miracle, he did not even need stones. Christ had created the world *ex nihilo*, out of nothing, so making a meal, even for a few thousand was hardly a test of his spiritual stamina.

The giving was not for His sake it was for the sake of the people. What ever message he preached that day the most poignant was the one that never left His lips: However little you are willing to give to Jesus he can make a lot out of it. It was a simple sermon and it was one that had already been preached many times before. Moses had heard it as he offered his shepherd's staff in the wilderness. Samson had become aware of it as he wielded the jawbone of an ass. David had learned it when he surrendered his sling into service.

We do not know what became of the boy. Of the four gospels only John takes the bother to mention him at all. What we can be sure of is this: that wherever he lived and grew into manhood there would not be a man in the town or village that would have the faith to match this. What a loss it would have been for him if he had not known the challenge of being willing to release the little that he had. What wealth he experienced in giving.

Willingness, or the lack of it, is a great watershed. Just before the dawn of the twentieth century a terrible disaster occurred on the river Thames. In dense fog the pleasure steamer *The Princess Alice* collided with the *Bywell Castle*. Of the nine hundred men, women and children that were jettisoned into the water six hundred perished. At the inquest two ferrymen gave evidence. The first is recorded as saying, 'I heard the crash and the cries but I thought, "Nobody knows I am here. I'm tired. I've done a hard day's work." I slipped home.' The second ferryman spoke thus, 'I got into my boat and pulled towards the scene of the disaster. When it was so full that I could not take another I cried, "O Lord for a bigger boat".'

I came across these words by Nathan C Schaeffer some time ago, 'At the close of life, the question will be not, "How much have you got?" but "How much have you given?" Not "How much have you won?" but "How much have you done?" Not "How much have you saved?" but "How much have you sacrificed?" It will be "How much have you loved and served?" not "How much were you honoured?" '

Open to Witness

If Christ is really dwelling within the heart of the Christian then this will be evidenced by a love for those who are not yet Believers. No one in their right mind, who really believes that there is a Hell, would want anyone to go there, especially anyone who they claim to love. Apart from this, knowing what Christ accomplishes in the life of the Believer in the 'here and now' should motivate every Born Again person to share their faith with those who do not yet know the Lord. Yet some seem willing to work in any sphere of service except that of personal Evangelism.

One of the most common reasons for this is fear. It is the anxiety that caused the disciples to cower behind locked doors after the crucifixion and prior to the day of Pentecost. It is a terrible 'no man's land' in which to live – knowing there is a message to tell but a sense of powerlessness to be able to proclaim it effectively. I have often tried to imagine what that scene was like.

'I wish I had a denarius for every time I said it would end up like this', gripes Thomas as he stares vacantly at the shuttered windows.

Philip is only half listening. Nobody ever gave a great deal of credence to what Thomas said. He was the sort of person who gave pessimism a bad name.

Matthew is in a world of his own. Still preoccupied with the option of returning to the tax office, he is turning over in his mind the possibility that there has been a change in the married man's personal allowance since he has been away.

All faces turn sympathetic to Peter when, for what seems like the hundredth time he rises to check that the door is locked. He looks like a man in a trance, haunted by a constant audio-visual replay of his own failure. Wherever he looks he meets the eyes of the Master as they engaged his own outside the Judgement Hall of Pilate. His ears are still ringing with the crowing of the cock that had stumbled, unwittingly, into prophecy.

Locked in their room, and even more deeply incarcerated by a sense of their own panic, if anyone needed a resurrection, the disciples did. It is hard to have open hearts behind locked doors.

They were not to know that at that very moment Satan too was in state of shock. He cowers, punch-drunk, in a corner of his private Hell. Certainly he had bruised the heel of the seed of the woman, but the head of the serpent had been sent reeling by a blow from which he was never to recover. Christ had conquered the grave and Satan had lost the keys to his own front door.

After the Day of Pentecost Peter is a different man. He stands up with the eleven instead of hiding with them. He raises his voice to speak instead of conducting his conversations in furtive whispers around a night watchman's fire. He addresses the crowd instead of trying ever so hard just to be one of them. The wind of Pentecost had blown away the shutters from their self-imposed prison. The fire of Pentecost had burned down the doors of their isolation from the world. He stood up with the eleven a different man: liberated, emancipated, free. Because he was open he was open to be open to others. Three thousand people were added to the church that day.

Two thousand years later Cedric, bowler hatted, walks blindly to the office like an automaton. He carries with him an air of deep-rooted apathy and briefcase in which he keeps his sandwiches. Mildred sits at her check-out till and stabs out her totals wearily. Her monotony is broken only by the occasional request for a carrier bag or change for a ten pound note.

Buried under a burden of responsibility and bound by the graveclothes of the mundane, Cedric and Mildred are in need of a resurrection too. Whether they are to get one remains to be seen. God had appeared to the disciples personally but he had delegated the responsibility of Cedric and Mildred to others. If they are to be reached it will be by twentieth century people with an open heart.

The Board of Deacons sit like inverted Micawbers. Waiting, not for something to turn up but for something to turn down. Once again there is no money for Evangelism as the financial balances are to be reserved for a 'rainy day'. The rainy day is guaranteed. They have been saving up for it for thirty years.

Mummified by lack of faith and atrophied by lack of action, along with their vision, the breath of God has gone. The smell of death is there and spiritual rigor mortis has set in – but can anyone be too dead for a resurrection. The answer, thankfully, is no.

The Apostle John said, 'When I saw him I fell at His feet as though dead. Then He placed his right hand on me and said, "I am the First and the Last. I am the living One: I was dead, and behold I am alive for ever and ever! and I hold the keys of death and Hades" .'[17]

If my heart is not open to witness I cannot blame the Devil for locking it, for as we have already seen, he has no keys that can imprison the Christian against their will and keep them bound.

If our hearts are closed to witness it is a sealing of our own doing and every one of us has as much power to be a released person as a 'closed' person in this respect. If I have a fear of 'what others will think of me' then I must come to terms with my pride and repent of it. If I have the kind of fear that is articulated by the phrase, 'I might not know what to say' then there are a multitude of 'Aids to Personal Evangelism' that can help to remedy this.

One reason offered why an individual might find it difficult to share their faith with their friends and colleagues might be, 'Well, it's not my nature to do that kind of thing. I'm an introvert and Evangelism is only for extroverts, isn't it?'

I used to think that that excuse was fair comment until I went to live next door to, the Quietest Man in the World.

My wife and I, newly married, moved into an end of terrace cottage in a little village called Cross Inn, South Wales. Though modernised to a certain degree it still had a flagstone kitchen floor, the significance of which will become apparent. Our neighbours were nice but very, very quiet. Often we would try to make conversation on those days when we were mowing our lawns or cutting the hedges. I don't know if the man next door ever gave more than two words and half a dozen grunts

103

in the first twelve months we lived there. He was the same with everybody. A nice man but quiet beyond belief. His hobby was Do-it-Yourself and one day he set his sights on making a new fitted kitchen for his wife. In order to do this his flagstone floor was to be broken up in order that a fresh concrete floor could be laid.

It was just about this time that we got a little labrador puppy. It was the kind that would do justice to any Andrex commercial.

Our neighbour had worked on his floor all day and by nightfall retired to bed leaving his kitchen door, which opened on to his garden, ajar in a probable attempt to facilitate the drying process.

We kept the usual routine that night. Shortly before retiring for bed we would bring in our dog from our garden and he would make his way to his basket in the corner of the kitchen.

Early next morning as we were having breakfast the doorbell rang. Who should it be but the Quietest Man in the World. Though quiet this time he wasn't. I don't think I have ever heard such eloquence. It seemed that on the previous night our dog had wandered beyond the boundaries of our garden into our neighbour's. From there he had found his kitchen door ajar. Fortunately the man next door had been unable to sleep that night, had come down to look at his handiwork and rectified the paw-mark patterns before the concrete had time to dry.

Our dog had become a catalyst. It had been the means of awakening a vast unknown vocabulary, stirring a new self-confidence. At last something had occurred that mattered enough to him to talk about. It may have been contrary to his normal nature but the excitement had smashed through the fear barrier and consequently the sound barrier had been broken too.

If such a thing can happen when a person has something, rightly, to complain about how much more when they have something exciting to witness about.

Jeremiah one day made a conscious decision not to speak of the things of God but was unable to abide by his resolve his reason being, 'His word is in my heart like a burning fire, shut up in my bones. I am weary of holding it in. Indeed I cannot.'[18]

Light always overcomes darkness – the darkness torch has yet to be invented. But although this is true, before the light can penetrate the world in which it is desperately needed it must first pass the frontiers of our own fear before it can become effective. Millions live under the heel of oppressive regimes, people who would speak openly if they could but cannot. It surely behoves us who are still free to speak, to do so while we can.

Incarcerated in the Nazi concentration camp, Corrie Ten Boom's friend, Betsy said, 'When we are set free we must do only one thing. We must take the Gospel over the whole world. We can tell of so much experience that is why people will listen. We can tell them that we have experienced that the light of Jesus is stronger than the deepest darkness.' One week later Betsy died.

It would, of course, be wrong to infer that the verbalisation of truth is the only form of witness that there is.

One day we were in a restaurant finishing our coffee when a woman approached us. She was tall, attractive and smiling. I certainly was not acquainted with her so I could only assume she was a friend of my wife, who was sitting next to me. As she came closer, the card she was carrying explained it all. She was modelling high-fashion rainwear on behalf of a large department store. Were we interested? It turned out that we were not, and she glided with the characteristic poise of a mannequin along the next aisle.

Secular modelling is based on the premise that in order to successfuly display beautiful things, you must first be beautiful yourself. The Spiritual parallel differs only slightly. Spiritually, in order to successfully display beautiful things one must be willing to become beautiful. The Apostle Paul writing to the Thessalonians, warning them against idleness and using himself as an example of a hard-worker writes, 'We did this not because we do not have the right to such help but in order for us to make ourselves a model for you to follow.' To Titus, giving instruction on how Christian employees should relate to their employers he says they should be encouraged to, '. . . show that they can be fully trusted, so that in every way they will make the teaching about God our Saviour attractive.

Making that which is beautiful, attractive is the model's job. It so sums up their whole mentality that they will submit to the most stoical dietry discipline to achieve it. Granted, for many their motives have more than a little to do with money and vanity, ego and cash-flow, but who would argue with their commitment?

The professing Christian who is not a model is a heretic – whatever he or she believes. It is a grave mistake to imagine that it is only the false cults, those who deny Christ doctrinally, who are religious deviants. To Titus, Paul writes of those who failed to be models and were, instead, 'mere talkers'. Of them, he says, 'They claim to know God, but *by their actions* deny Him. On the understanding that we are going to be judged according to the light that we have received, who is to be the better off: a person who does not believe in that and lives badly, or a person who claims to believe in the judgement of God and behaves badly? He who believes wrong is certainly wrong, but he who claims to believe right, and lives wrong, must be doubly in error.

Truth must lead to godliness if it is to lead anywhere at all. Anything less creates a caricature of the Christian and a travesty of the truth. The Gospel has to be modelled in order that its impact may not be lost. The Seventeenth century Puritan, Richard Baxter, in his book *The Reformed Pastor* used a culinary example: 'Though you know the meat to be good and wholesome, yet it may make a weak stomach rise against it if the cook or the servant that carrieth it hath leprous or even dirty hands.'

Sandwiched between the illustrations from Thessalonians and Titus is Paul's testimony to Timothy. Whilst describing himself as the worst of sinners he significantly remarks, 'But for that very reason I was shown mercy so that in me Christ Jesus might *display* His unlimited patience as an example for those who would believe.'

The distinction between secular and spiritual modelling may seem small but it is a vital one. God did not choose us because we were beautiful but that we might become beautiful. In the secular sense the model and the merchandise are two separate entities. In the spiritual realm the model and the display are necessarily linked. When Paul speaks of Christ displaying something IN him, that is exactly what he means.

Jesus, as always the ultimate example, not only displayed the fruit of the Spirit, He was, and of course is, the embodiment of it. He was never a guidepost; He is ever the Guide. He chose His Disciples not, we read, that they might listen to Him, but that they might be with Him. That is what discipleship is all about.

If a Gestapo officer and a KGB agent could be rolled into one then the end product would be a fairly accurate portrait of Paul prior to his conversion. Was the title he gives himself, 'Chief of Sinner' a display of mega-modesty or hyper-humility? It is hardly likely that we would have thought so if we had been forced to cower under his sadistic henchmen as their evil instruments of torture encouraged us to blaspheme. Had he remained unconverted he would have had to stand, like those in a later Nuremberg, to answer for war crimes against the people of God. Incredibly, this man, of all men, was ripe for recruitment into God's modelling agency. God had displayed patience with him and now was to display His patience through him.

What innovative management it was that took the raincoat from the lifeless dummy in the showcase and put it on the living model that could walk among the people. Yet such an action pales into insignificance when compared to the divine Mind that decreed that the Word be made flesh and live among us.

On reflection, I am surprised that I did not recognise the woman in the restaurant straight away. After all, you can always tell a model by the way she walks. So too the Christian.

Probably the finest book I have ever read on the subject of Personal Evangelism is *Life-Style Evangelism* by Joseph Aldrich. In it he speaks of the balance between what we say and how we live, in terms of a song. The lyrics are the spoken truths of the Gospel, the way we live is the music. He points out that Peter[19] illustrates the power of 'music' when he encourages wives with spiritually indifferent husbands to, 'Shut off the words and play the music. The power of a changed life is presented as a strategic means of winning those who are spiritually indifferent.' He later says, 'Evangelism is sterophonic. God speaks to his creatures through two channels: the written Word, and you, His 'living epistle'. God's redemptive love is declared in Scripture, demonstrated at the Cross, and displayed in the body.'[20]

All too often the word 'holiness' conjures up a mental picture of that which is dull and drab and creates an image of people who are hard and austere. Nothing could be further from the truth. Holiness is attractive. the most holy people I have ever known have also been the most approachable people I have ever known. Samuel Chadwick once said, 'To witness, is to live in such a way that our lives would not make sense if God did not exist.'

Many years ago I attended the funeral of an elderly Baptist minister. He had been converted way back in the Welsh Revival and had pastored the church in the same village for no less than forty yers before retiring. It was in his retirement that I first came to know him. He and his wife were beautiful and Godly people. A story told at the funeral by a life long friend of his, will ever remain in my mind.

On one occasion he had been speaking at a church Convention outside of Wales. A lady had entered the service late. She was not a Christian at that point, and she too was a visitor to that area. The message had a great impression on her and she went home with the firm resolve to surrender herself to Christ. As a result, her life was completely transformed and she longed to get in touch with the minister whose message had had such an impact upon her life. The problem was that she knew neither his name or address. All she could remember was that he had been introduced as a man who lived in the village of Llantrisant. Undaunted she wrote the letter and addressed it to 'The Man of God, Llantrisant'. The speaker at the funeral service told the congregation that the letter had reached the minister. His Open Witness was such that, not just his congregation, but the Postman too knew the calibre of the man.

One of the lesser known titles of the people of God is that of a people who are 'Sought After'.[21] This is the hallmark of holiness. It refers to those whose verbal witness may seem to be being ignored by those around but, when non-Christian colleagues, family and friends face problems or trauma, it is they who are their first resource. They possess a holiness characterised by warmth, sincerity and integrity. Their lives have been watched under the microscopic scrutiny of unconverted eyes and have passed the test. As 'epistles' they have been read and the content of their faith has been seen to be fact and not fiction. It is significant that one of the Bible words to describe a clean life, *Katharos*, is used classically of a document that has been corrected and is now 'free of errors'. It is the word of a corrected proof.

It is the Christian who shows no cracks when subjected to the wind-tunnel of affliction that has the greatest impact on a world that has, as yet, not discovered God. Nobody is impressed by a person who claims to have supernatural revelation and an indwelling divine dynamic but who collapses under pressure far more easily than a person who does not claim to be a Christian. It is at the point, however small and insignificant to us, that we can cope when others can't, that the message begins to get through.

This truth is nowhere more pertinently revealed than in the account of Aaron and the Magicians.[22] Every plague that had come upon Egypt to that point the magician had been able to reconstruct through the occult arts. When the plague of gnats arose they found themselves powerless to copy it. All at once their cynicism turned to conviction. Their report to Pharaoh was worded thus, 'This is the finger of God.' Imagine it, converted by a fly. The evidence may have been minute but the signficance was gigantic.

We live in a day when homosexuals adorn themselves with badges which declare them to be 'Glad to be Gay'. Though their deviatonary practices are everywhere in Scripture declared to be an abomination in the eyes of God they encourage one another to 'come out' and declare themselves proudly. With our society in such a state now is not the time for Closet Christians.

Joseph of Arimathea is known as being a 'secret disciple' – another phrase which is a contradition in terms. As he witnessed the crucifixion he became weary of the social camouflage that had kept him conveniently blended into the background. Jesus hanging in open shame challenged him to witness with an open heart. It was time for Joseph to declare himself whatever the cost. He could have not chosen a more public 'Coming Out' occasion than he did. He decided that he would nail his colours to the mast by approaching Pilate and ask for the body of Jesus. It was a big moment for Joseph, his whole future was on the line. He decided not to go alone. He took someone else with him – someone who had gone through the very same conflict that he had endured, a person also willing to pay the price.

For me, John 19:38–40 is one of the most moving passages in the New Testament.

Later, Joseph of Arimathea asked Pilate for the body of Jesus, but secretly because he feared the Jews. With Pilate's permission, he came and took the body. He was accompanied by Nicodemus, the man who earlier had visited Jesus at night.

Open to One Another

The writings of Moses supply us with an intriguing insight into the decision making processes of the Old

111

Testament High Priests. 'Whenever Aaron enters the Holy Place, he will bear the names of the sons of Israel over his heart on the breastpiece of decision as a continual memorial before the Lord. Also put the Urim and Thummim in the breastpiece, so they may be over Aaron's heart whenever he enters the presence of the Lord. Thus Aaron will always bear the means of making decisions for the Israelites over his heart before the Lord.'[23]

God, through this symbolism, was revealing to His people that he was looking for spiritual leadership that would 'feel' for those they were responsible for. They were not to make bureaucratic decisions based merely on accumulated knowledge.

We have already had occasion to note the fickleness of the human heart. It is the cauldron in which moods and temperaments continually simmer. Our 'heart' towards someone today may differ radically from our attitude to them at some time in the future. This is surely why the passage adds, 'before the Lord'.

The High Priest, when challenged to make a decision on behalf of the people, could not get away with the subjective response, 'It will depend how I feel at the time.' He was called to administer a justice based upon how God would feel at the time. He was conscious that when it came to relationships they were 'the people of God' first and 'his people' second. The Apostle Paul exemplifies this in a New Testament sense when he says, 'We have spoken freely to you Corinthians, and opened wide our hearts to you.'[24]

When we begin to grasp the truth of how important individual people are to God we are drawn to the conclusion that we need to be very careful how we treat one another.

If someone were entrusted by a friend to look after a

priceless painting while they were abroad three things would be fixed in their mind as continual reference points. The first would be that they would need to watch the environment in which the painting is housed to ensure that no damage is done to the work of art. Secondly, they would be aware that they will be accountable for its condition on their friend's return. Lastly they will be conscious of the fact that should some calamity have occurred during the time it was in their care the relationship between their friend and themselves would be affected.

When Cain asked God. 'Am I my brother's keeper?' it was not a serious question and in consequence did not provoke a direct reply. The New Testament clearly teaches that followers of Jesus have been made members one of another. Evangelicals in the past have strongly, and rightly, promoted the truth that God does not see His church as merely a corporate mass of mankind but that each individual has a personal relationship with Christ. The danger lies in the overemphasis of that fact. It must not be forgotten that the Lord continually monitors our professed love for Him in the light of our expressed love for one another.[25]

The value of a painting, however significant a work of art it may be, is reduced at auction to monetary terms. Each individual Believer has been redeemed not with 'silver or gold' but with the blood of Jesus. From the cross Jesus entrusted the care of his mother to John with the words, 'Woman behold thy son.' In no lesser a way does God entrust us to the care of one another. 'Behold your brother. Behold your sister', He says.

We are accountable to God for the stewardship of our relationships. Our fellow Christian may be a merchant banker or a converted gypsy. To God each has been bought with a price and each is equally precious. The commitment to 'one another' is comprehensive. The Scripture spells it out. Honour one another. Be like-minded toward one another. Accept one another. Serve one another. Carry one another's burdens. Forgive one another. Encourage one another. Offer hospitality to one another. Spur one another on. Confess your faults to one another. Pray for one another. Love one another.[26]

Right relationship is the true fabric of real community. When Jesus chose His disciples He did it with a developing relationship in mind more than anything else. As we have noted in an earlier chapter, the Scripture records that He did not choose them primarily so that He could teach or preach to them but that they might be 'with Him'. Though they gleaned from His preaching, parables and prophecies nothing in all their encounter with Him was more telling or more eloquent than the language of his life lived under the magnifying lens of their perpetual gaze. Though they were servants, subjects and sons He also takes great delight in calling them friends.[27]

To be open hearted to one another means that we will be especially open hearted towards the vulnerable.

The last church meeting that Paul had in Ephesus was memorable in more ways than one. He was to leave early the next day and, knowing he would probably never see them again, the meeting went on late – so late in fact, that at midnight he was still preaching.

The people were meeting in a third floor room. It was packed to capacity to the degree that people were even sitting on the open window ledges. The largeness of the crowd, combined with the fumes from the many oil lamps that were burning, meant that the atmosphere was becoming very stuffy. Some, not surprisingly, were beginning to fall asleep. One young man 'dropped off' literally – not just to sleep, but from his precarious position on the window ledge. He was killed by the fall but after prayer was miraculously restored to life. The Scripture then records that Paul recommenced his message and preached until daylight.

Eutychus did not enter the meeting place that day with the express purpose of throwing himself from the window. What happened to him literally was something that, in a spiritual sense, happens to people all the time. He took up his position on the edge of the congregation and, imperceptibly, he became more and more vulnerable as time went by. Lots of fellow Christians were huddled around him in the crowd but because they were all intent on 'getting what they could out of the meeting' they remained unaware that someone near them was slipping away.

In Fellowships large and small there are those who live on the perimeter of things. It is often assumed that because they are present at services and celebrations that all is well with their soul. Their condition may be amply camouflaged by chorus singing but in reality they are 'falling away'.

When Eutychus fell a miracle brought him to life. Not all who fall are so fortunate. A fence at the top of a cliff is far better than an ambulance at the bottom. The Open Hearted have an eye for the vulnerable. They seek to build them into the body.

It has been rightly pointed out that when the Bible uses the analogy of the Church as a building it speaks of those who are fitted together. We are mortised not mortared. We are built together not stuck together. Only an open heart towards others can bring this about.

Not to live in relationship can cause the Christian to succumb to what I choose to call the Laish Syndrome. It sounds like a terrible disease and in a way it is. It is marked by three pernicious elements, and over the years

I have known more than one whose spiritual life has been rendered totally ineffective through it. In most cases it does not prove to be fatal if caught early enough, though it has to be said, everyone in the Church is a potential sufferer.

The town of Laish was a nondescript place. It would not have found itself etched into even the guidebooks of the Old Testament days. Its inhabitants were self-assured to the point of naivety. Had the town ever had a motto it would have been, 'It could never happen to us'. The Scripture simply refers to them prior to the Danites putting the whole community to the sword and burning the city to the ground as, 'A peaceful and unsuspecting people'.

The rubble-strewn remains of the town lies as perpetual and monumental memorial to 'vulnerability'. Of Laish, Judges 18:28 records: 'There was no one to rescue them because they lived a long way from Sidon and had no relationship with anyone else. The city was in a valley near Beth Rehob.'

They were Geographically vulnerable. They lived a long way from Sidon.

Much is said, and rightly so, about the sacrifice made by Missionaries who, 'leave home and family for the sake of the Gospel'. What is sometimes forgotten is that a Pastor and his wife, especially in the early part of their ministry, accepting a call to a church just a few hundred miles away from their home roots can feel, in reality, on the other side of the world.

More often than not it is the minister's wife that feels the wrench the most. The pastor, throwing himself into the challenge, meeting new people and opportunities on a day-to-day basis, is in some way anaesthetised to the real sense of severance pain. His helpmeet on the other hand, engrossed as she often is with the responsibility of the family unit, lives with the constant reminder of family far away. It needs to be noticed that spiritual leaders are not immune from the disease either and, in some ways, they are the most vulnerable of all. They are not called to build a building at 'arms length'. They are part of the construction themselves.

Those within the local congregation who live some distance from where the church meets and cannot easily find fellowship with other Christians because of distance, lack of transport or other reasons are legitimate love-targets for the Open Hearted. An occasional dose of hospitality helps to keep this symptom of the virus well in check.

They were Emotionally vulnerable. They had no relationship with anyone.

Any church that is effectively reaching the community will be bringing into its embrace the lonely, the hurting, the alienated and the oppressed, those recently divorced or endeavouring to bring up children alone.

Loneliness knows no socio-economic boundaries. Many who have reached the top of their profession have done so at the expense of the cultivation of long term relationships. It may be because their chosen career has moved them around or that their field of responsibility has called upon them to work long and 'unsocial hours'.

Whatever the reason and whoever is hurting the Lord has a healing word. It is spoken by the Psalmist when he says, 'God sets the lonely in families, He leads forth the prisoners with singing: but the rebellious life in a sun scorched land.'[28]

A marginal reading has 'He gives the desolate a homeland'. Who knows more what desolation is about more than those who have been deserted. Moffat translates it, 'He brings the lonely home.' Another has it

117

'He brings the lonely into relationship.' If the Church fails to be a homeland for the lonely then, quite simply, it has failed. There are some churches that pride themselves on their technological precision but are sadly lacking when one looks for a sense of community or a feeling of warmth.

Michael Griffiths puts it so well when he says, 'To fight for merely doctrinal faithfulness is like the wife who never sleeps with anyone else but never shows love to her own husband. The call is not only to be the bride faithful, but the bride in love.'[29]

One of the most stirring pictures of the Open Heart of Jesus is revealed when He weeps over Jerusalem with the words, 'O Jerusalem, Jerusalem . . . how often I longed to gather your children together, as a hen gathers her chicks under her wings, but you were not willing.'[30]

Jesus was expressing here two very separate, yet related, points. The first was that He was calling them to Himself. The second was that He was, by that act, calling them together. Certainly 'chickens under the wing' may on occasions tread on one another's toes but that was little price to pay for the benefits of real relationship and the security from prowling predators who seek out those who choose to walk independently. Jesus was teaching the impossibility of being a disciple in isolation.

Certainly, not all are willing to be built into relationship. There are those who will rebel against it, and for them the Lord also has a word, 'They will live in a sun scorched land.' Some would argue that they:

a) *Don't have the Need*
If Jesus saw the need to cultivate relationships, though the Creator and the Master of the Universe, then how can we his children act as if we are wiser.

b) *Don't have the Time*

Then time should be made. Jesus did. If we are too busy to cultivate deep relationships then we are too busy. It is not just a matter of 'relaxing with people' from time to time. It is the vital knowledge that there are those around you who will love you enough to tell you the truth about yourself – for better or worse – people who will speak into your life because they want God's best for you as you want God's best for them.

They were Positionally vulnerable. The city was in a valley.

Everybody could see them without being seen themselves. It was the typical 'Goldfish bowl' effect. The people of Laish were unaware of the many hundreds of eyes staring down at them from the surrounding hillsides. Their valley-position, however, was far more disadvantageous for strategically it was the worst possible vantage point. They were 'down' while everyone else was 'up'. A precarious and depressing position that would be experienced by not a few Christians who would live in the centuries that would follow.

Many in our society are vulnerable because of the defenceless 'position' they are in. Statistics of crimes against the child and against the elderly are continually on the increase.

Open Hearted Christians of the past have done much to act as salt and light in the community to bring about radical change in the social order. Their lives display the vital characteristics of those who are truly Open. The Open Hearted are not sentimental: they are strong and often very courageous.

Numbered amongst those, in the past, who are remembered as having a heart for others would be

Wilberforce in his bringing about the abolition of slavery, The Early of Shaftesbury and the Factory Act, Kier Hardie and the Labour Movement, Elizabeth Fry and Prison Reform.

These people knew nothing of the Hermit Theology embraced by some Christians who see 'Separation' solely in terms of isolation from the real world; They were of the calibre of Lord Cairnes of whom it is said that whenever he entered the House, however late and however poisonous the atmosphere, his very presence brought peace and harmony. Little wonder. He spent two hours in prayer every day before going to Parliament.

Contemporary examples are seen in the vigilance of Mary Whitehouse and the clear and open testimony of those who work within the Arts, The Media, and the Entertainment Industry.

It is perhaps remarkable that those Christians who speak most about the decadence of the Film Industry, poor quality television and the secularism of politics are often also the ones who have discouraged their sons and daughters from training as Directors and Producers and entering politics, on the premise that such occupations are far too 'worldly. One cannot have one's cake and eat it. It's hard to be holy and hide.

The most defenceless individual of all is the unborn child. Those Christians who rise up against abortion and give the voiceless a vocabulary and articulate their 'silent scream' are Believers with an Open Heart. Those Christians within with CARE, SPUC, LIFE, and other caring pressure groups, are certainly cases in point.

Vital as doctrine is, it needs to be noted that it is the Church, not theology, that the Apostle Paul describes as being the, 'pillar and foundation of the truth'.[31]

Surgery is usually seen as a last resort. When the initial tell-tale signs of heart trouble are diagnosed the doctor is more likely to prescribe a change in diet or life-style than he is to refer the patient directly to a hospital consultant for treatment.

All that we have said in this chapter so far as had to do with a health regime for the heart. If all a Christian does is to sit like sermon fodder in the pew and feed, feed, feed and seldom takes the opportunity to 'exercise their faith' they will soon become overweight and a prime candidate for one of the many spiritual diseases of the heart. Often a change in diet and a willingness to exercise does the trick. Sometimes the situation is so acute that only the surgeon's scalpel will suffice.

Even though the treatment can be painful there are those who call upon God for an operation – whatever it might entail. 'Create in me a pure heart', said David, and later in the same Psalm, 'A broken and a contrite heart, O God, you will not despise.'[32]

David had suffered from a severe hardening of the arteries. Seeing himself a supreme ruler he had become immune to the overtures of the Holy Spirit to his conscience and had consequently fallen into sin. God appointed the prophet Nathan to diagnose his condition. It was to be a painful time for David with very little in the way of anaesthetic to dull his discomfort. Yet God had made a new man of him. It was worth it all in the end. He was to find out by experience that God really was, 'Close to the broken-hearted and saves those who are crushed in spirit'[33] for whatever reason. David discovered that God's surgical skill, though often painful, is always conducted in the context of His 'intensive care'.

There are three characteristic symptoms of the heart that needs urgent surgery. They are found in people who have ignored the warning signs and whose spiritual experience has been limited by their disease.

The Hardness that impedes Unction

When Jesus was about to heal the man with the withered hand He noticed the sullen spectators that surrounded Him. The Scriptures say that He was angry at the hardness and stubborness of their hearts. He sought for faith and all he got was bleak looks. Their spiritual disease, like so many that are physical, could be seen in their faces. Those of which Jesus spoke were religious, committed, and dedicated to the Law, knowledgeable and hard.

The Hardness that impedes Action

William Barclay has pointed out that the Greek word used for hardness of heart, *porosis*, refers to the chalk stone that forms in the joints and paralyses action.[34] The hard-hearted are seldom known for their achievement. Their lives do not attract others to Christ. They may be known for their hard lines but rarely for their accomplishments.

The Hardness that impedes Vision

It is sometimes assumed that if more miracles took place within the Church more people would be drawn to it. That may well be true but it cannot be taken for granted. Many of the miracles that Jesus performed were not only lost on the crowd, they were lost on the disciples too. They could experience a supernatural act in their lives yesterday but were totally unable to believe God for today. Mark, referring to a period of stress they went through says of them, 'They had not understood about the loaves; (the miracle of the feeding of the five thousand) their hearts were hardened.'[35] What God had done previously had made no 'impression' on them. The Greek philosophers believed that the mind was like a wax tablet on which impressions were made. Hard hearts were therefore not teachable hearts.

Most of us are aware of the time when Jeremiah went down to the potter's house and saw a vessel which was marred in the potter's hands being remodelled into something that was beautiful – an operation only possible because of the softness and malleability of the clay. What is not always noticed is that God sent Jeremiah a second time to the Potter and what happens is recorded in the next chapter of his book. This time the pot is not remade but is smashed instead. It had become hardened to change. Sometimes all that God can do with hard things, and hard hearts, is to break them.

I remember on one occasion having a meal with a leading member of another denomination, and asking about the well-being of his son, a contemporary of mine who I had not seen for some years.

My friend told me how his son had got married but within just a few years the relationship had broken up. The girl had left him for someone else. His son was now living alone. I almost wished I had not asked the question. It was clear that what had happened had brought the family very deep pain.

He paused for a moment before continuing. As he turned his head towards me I could see that his eyes had moistened. 'John,' he said, 'I'm approaching retirement now and I can't help but think of all the young men that have come into my office over the years with problems similar to those that have affected my son. If I could live my time over again I would never have been so hard. Perhaps the decisions I made then and the conclusions I came to would not have altered greatly, but oh, I would have dealt with them ever so differently. You never expect these things to come to your door, and when it does, it breaks you.'

I felt that he was trying to tell me something and teach me something at the same time. I resolved to try and learn and could not help but bring to mind the words of Job when he said, 'The Lord makes my heart soft, for the Almighty troubleth me'.[36]

It was in Cape Town, 1967, that Christian Barnard conducted the first human heart transplant. Louis Washkansky, the recipient, must have felt very much part of the quantum leap that medical science had made during that period. He may or may not have been aware that two thousand five hundred and sixty years earlier God had announced His intention to give new hearts simultaneously to a whole Nation and, for the past two thousand years, has been not only providing new hearts but creating a Kingdom of new people.[37]

The Rule of the Open Heart

Paul's prayer for the Ephesian church was that Christ might dwell in their heart by faith. The idea is one of taking up permanent residence in the centre of their being. God always wants to be at the very centre of His people.

When He created man He walked with him in the Garden. When the people of Israel journeyed through the wilderness He ordained that the tabernacle was to be in the centre of the camp. When we turn to the last book of the Bible we see the Church portrayed as seven golden lampstands and John, as he observes the vision, notices someone walking amongst them. It is none other than Christ Himself.

It is not merely the purpose of Christ to dwell in the heart but to rule in the heart. If the Prince of Peace takes up residence in the centre of a life we can assume that it is peace that will be the most obvious characteristic of His reign.

Peace is a rare commodity. In less than eight per cent of history, from the beginning of recorded time, has the world been entirely at peace. In a total of three thousand five hundred and thirty years only two hundred and eighty six of them have been warless. No less than eight thousand international treaties have been broken during that period.

World tension, however, is just an enlargement of the tension within the human heart. Shrapnel may destroy a home from without but selfishness will destroy a home from within. It has been jokingly said that there is such stress in society at the present time that if Moses had come down from the mountain today the tablets he would be carrying would be Panadols.

Whilst we recognise the problem, the Christian is also aware of the antidote – an Open Heart in which God rules and reigns. The Devil has other ideas for us but, then again, he always has.

Space Invader machines have died and now gather dust. They have largely disappeared as quickly as they came, cobwen-ridden, into the black hole of microchip antiquity. Peace Invaders however are here to stay, at least that is until Jesus returns. How successful they are in their onslaught depends on a number of factors.

If we can know something of the origin, nature and tactics of any enemy then our foe is already on the way to an ignominious defeat. This is as true on the spiritual battlefield as it is in any other martial scenario, be it a chess-board or a nuclear theatre of war.

Satan is a destroyer. He has nominated every expression of the fruit of the Spirit as a legitimate target for attack but amongst the highest on his hit list is peace. Peace, that precious jewel that Matthew Henry, the seventeenth century commentator, said he would exchange anything for but truth.

The maxim, 'You are nearer God's heart in a garden than anywhere else on Earth', is probably true of only two gardens in history. The first is the Garden of Eden before the Fall and the other, significantly, the Garden of Gethsemane where the consequences of the Fall were being reversed.

When man fell he was separated from God and his peace was shattered. This act brought into being the first spiritual, sociological, psychological and ecological problems. The broken pieces of peace would never again be gathered up, let alone mended, until Calvary, at which time peace would be 'made' by Christ's blood on the Cross.[39]

It is impossible to grasp the meaning of inner peace provided by the indwelling presence of the Holy Spirit until we begin to understand the peace made possible by the master Mediator of Golgotha's hill.

Modern day mediators, be they international or industrial, contribute little else to the reconciliation process other than their expertise and advice. No one would expect ACAS, for example, to provide from their own resources the wherewithal to settle a pay dispute. But of Jesus, Isaiah prophesies, 'The punishment that brought us peace was upon Him'[40] The designation 'Prince of Peace' was no hereditary title.

Through Christ, peace is a real possibility for every child of God. The Psalmist says that, 'God blesses His people with peace.' To His disciples Jesus said, 'Peace I leave with you; my peace I give you. I do not give to you as the world gives. Do not let your hearts be troubled and do not be afraid.'[41]

Peace was announced at the birth of Jesus. It was left,

before His death, as a legacy to a restless world and was the subject matter of the announcement made to the disciples by the risen Lord. God does not play 'cat and mouse' with us. He does not tantalise us with the unobtainable.

Ideally there needs to be a buffer zone between the individual and what we have called the Peace Invader. In fact there is. The Amplified Version of Philippians 4:7 reads, 'And God's peace be yours, that tranquil state of a soul assured of its salvation through Christ, and so fearing nothing from God and content with its earthly lot of whatever sort that is, that peace which transcends all understanding, shall garrison and mount guard over your hearts and minds in Christ Jesus.

In real terms this means that the enemy of our souls must fight past the armed guard at the gates before he can reach us. Before we can be affected the garrison first has to be overcome. Potentially we are as peaceful as God, for the peace that is keeping God is keeping us.

As the mind is the gateway to the heart it is vital that the mind is in subjection to the authority of Christ. To the Romans Paul writes, 'The mind controlled by the Spirit is life and peace', or to use Isaiah's words, 'You will keep in perfect peace him whose mind is steadfast, because he trusts in you.'[42]

A mind controlled is a mind in submission. To live outside obedience is a recipe for tension. We become, as H G Wells once described one of his characters, 'Not so much a person but more a civil war.'

It has been said that when our will crosses God's will then our will must die. We cannot expect to 'take God on' and win. Peace is the deliberate adjustment of our life to the will of God. It is obedience arising, not from the coercion of legalism, but from a willing disposition. 'Great peace', says the Psalmists, 'have they who love Thy law.' Duty is not substitute for love.

God's peace is 'Shalom Peace'. It is wholeness, completeness and harmony. It is peace that encompasses body, soul and spirit. In the Gospel of Luke Jesus spoke peace to a sinful woman – peace for the spirit. He spoke peace to a sick woman – peace for the body. He spoke peace to a storm – the stressful situations that trouble the soul.[43]

To the church in Colossae Paul said, 'Let the peace of Christ rule in your hearts.' He has created the Open Hearted to be his Peace People.

6: The Open Mind

Our emotions express how we feel; our mind expresses what we think and our will communicates what we want.

To possess a mind that is fully open to God will mean that the seat of our intellect will be closed to a number of other things. This is why those who are the most open minded towards God appear to be the most narrow minded as far as the world is concerned.

This arises from a basic difference in definition of what constitutes the 'Open Mind'. The minds of some appear to be so open they can seem empty. Such people pride themselves not on their faith but on their doubts. Their's is a sophisticated 'spirituality' that rejoices in what they do not know. Conviction is dubbed dogmatism and any strong stance is declared as bigotry. Absolutes are sneered at and grey areas are forever the 'colour of the month'. For them, Christianity is punctuated with question marks. Exclamation marks are conspicuous by their absence.

A multitude of complicated issues do not lend themselves to the simplistic colour separation of black and white. Yet it is the certainty about those things of which we can be sure that bring such blurred images into sharper focus.

Before one can begin to understand the implications of the Open Mind the concept of the Renewed Mind must first be addressed. To the church at Rome Paul writes, 'Be not conformed to the world but be transformed by the renewing of your mind. Then you churches that I had ever pastored to that date. They will be able to test and approve what God's will is – His good, pleasing and perfect will.'[1]

I have never met a Christian who does not want to know the will of God in their life. The Bible says that the secret to it is found in the renewed mind. The Scripture further reveals that, potentially, every Christian has the 'mind of Christ'.[2] Subsequent to New Birth, the secular mind-set and Godless thought-forms are remodelled through communion with Christ and the mind enters into a state of renewal. There is a saying that you get to look like the people you live with. Whether that is true or not may be debatable; what we can be sure about is that the longer one spends quality time in the presence of God the more likely one is to understand and appreciate His purposes.

From time to time one meets the type of Christian who is for ever seeking The Will of God waiting for some special message or blinding flash or revelation. The nature of my ministry requires me to spend a high proportion of my time travelling. The only time that I ask for directions is when I am lost. Having set my destination most of my journey is spent in noticing signs that confirm that I am on the right road.

The Believer with a mind that is open for God's word to be communicated to them via a consistent devotional life, public ministry, fellowship and spiritual gifts should, with all that data at their disposal, be able to discern God's purposes for them on a day to day basis. The renewed mind comes about through a process of submissive listening. It is the product of communion.

The state of our health is to a large extent a product of the balance of our diet. The state of our soul is directly affected by that which our mind feeds upon.

'Those who live according to the sinful nature have their minds set on what that nature desires; but those who live in accordance with the Spirit have their minds set on what the Spirit desires. The mind of sinful man is death but the mind controlled by the Spirit is life and peace' Romans 8:5,6.

This is the reason why the Open Mind towards God must post a sentry to guard itself from that which would subvert it, destroy its peace and undermine its faith. The Renewed Mind examines every thought and submits it to the challenge, 'Friend or Foe?' To the Corinthian church Paul writes, 'We take captive every thought and make it obedient to Christ.'[3] J B Phillips paraphrases this as, 'We fight to capture every thought until it acknowledges the authority of Christ.'

Paul gave the calorie counter to the church at Corinth, a warning concerning additives to the church at Rome, and the diet sheet to the church at Philippi, 'Whatever is true, whatever is noble, whatever is right, whatever is pure, whatever is lovely, whatever is admirable – if anything is excellent or praiseworthy – think about such things.'[4]

Two strong bolts challenge the emancipation that is always experienced when a mind is fully Open to God.

The Challenge of Intransigence

Most of us are aware of the old cliché, 'The seven last words of a dying church are, "We have always done it this way" ' or 'If you dig a rut deep enough it becomes a grave' but the question that has to be addressed is, 'Why do people, even those of us who profess to want to follow the Lord, find change such a difficult thing to come to terms with?'

131

There are very few people who, if they are honest, are not willing to contemplate the possibility that there is a better way of doing something than the way they are operating at the present time. Only if I can categorically say that that which I am currently engaged in is God's last word on the matter can I close my mind to anything else. One does come across the occasional Christian, or group of Christians, who give you the distinct impression that they have 'got it all'. It is ever so hard at such times to not succumb to the temptation to ask the question, 'If you have got it all, then where is it all?'

Obviously not everything that is new is a change for the better. On the other hand the Believer has to recognise the fact that change is part of the process of discipleship. It is hard to be a 'follower' if I am constantly standing still.

In the thirty-second Psalm the Lord says, 'I will instruct you and teach you in the way that you should go: I will counsel and watch over you. Do not be like the horse or the mule, which have no understanding but must be controlled by bit and bridle or they will not come to you.'

Wherever there is growth there is change. Ask any parent. If we are 'Changing from one degree of glory to another' then change is inevitable. When a house-plant reaches a certain stage of its growth a new structure, a pot, must be found to accommodate it – otherwise its very development will be the cause of its death. The whole of God's creation cries out for change both to accommodate and facilitate growth.

I read an article recently that revealed a remarkable thing about the life of a shark. Apparently, if a small shark is caught and confined, it will stay a size proportionate to the aquarium in which it is housed. It is possible in this way for a shark to be nine inches long yet fully matured. Yet if it is turned loose in time, into the ocean, it will grow to its normal length of eight feet.

Far too many of us consider ourselves to be fully developed when we, like the nine inch shark, are only a shadow of what God created us to be.

Change can be resisted simply because of the way it is presented and understood. The difficult thing for most of us is not the acceptance of something new: it is the assumption that by doing so we are rejecting something old. That which is now considered 'old' may have been the means of bringing great blessing to us in years gone by. It almost seems sacrilegious to even consider change in such circumstances and we say, 'If God has blessed us in the past then how can that which we were engaged in have been so wrong?'

This misunderstanding is the biggest challenge to constructive change. It is based on the false premise that, 'If the new is right, the old must be wrong.' The logic then seems to follow, 'If I know the old was not wrong then the new cannot be right.'

Harmony can be achieved when we understand that God's word is a Proceeding Word. An event in the life of Elijah illustrates the point.

In 1 Kings 17 God called Elijah to the Kerith Ravine. God told him to drink from the brook and ravens would come and bring him bread. God not only called him but chose the means to sustain him.

Later in the chapter we read that God called him again and told him to go to Zarephath. Elijah the Tishbite had two possible responses to this request for change.

He could have questioned the request on the grounds that God had called him to the brook in the past and the evidence of that call was seen in the way that God had blessed his obedience by supplying his needs. If that had been his response he would have died by a dry, raven-free ravine, the last words on his parched lips being, 'The new word cannot be right because the old word brought such miracles.'

The action he decided to take demonstrated that he could embrace the new thing that God was saying without, in any way, rejecting the way that God had dealt with him in the past. Miracles in the past there most certainly had been, but miracles there were yet to be, accompanying his new obedience.

It can be extremely difficult for the best of us to say 'Yes' to change when we have been saying 'No' to it for so long. Whether we can do it or not depends largely on our spiritual stature. God deliver us from defending the *status quo* when all we are really doing is defending our own pride.

Mark McCormack tells in his book, *What They Don't Teach You At The Harvard Business School*, that a circus keeps a baby elephant from running away by chaining it to a stake. When the animal pulls the chain, the cuff chafes its leg and the baby elephant concludes that to avoid pain it is best to stay put. But when the elephant grows up it is still chained to the same small stake. The mature elephant can now pull the stake out of the ground like a tooth pick, but the elephant remembers the pain and does not use the new set of facts. In this way the tiny stake keeps the two ton elephant at bay just as effectively as it did the baby.

What we did yesterday has to be viewed in the light of today. The conclusion of a renewed and open mind may see no need whatsoever for altering course. If it does it should. Flexibility must be supported. Ruts must be resisted.

One of the most interesting secular books that I have ever read is entitled, *In Search of Excellence*. It is a three

134

hundred and sixty page analysis of America's best run companies. Toward the end of the book the two writers conclude, 'We believe that if an organisation is to meet the challenge of a changing world, it must be prepared to change everything about itself except those things that it believes.'

There are some that would argue that the Church has nothing to learn from the world. Jesus would not agree. To our shame He says, 'For the people of this world are more shrewd in dealing with their own kind than are the people of the light'.[5] When we consider that Henry Ford, the inventor of the massed produced motor car, once said that he took the Church's survival as a sign of God's existence for no other enterprise, run so poorly, could ever stay in business: we might conclude that we might have more to learn yet.

A large Baptist church in Sale, Cheshire, has the following statement in their membership course.

'At the heart of our Fellowship's life is a desire and determination to live under the lordship (the kingly, authoritative, decision rule) of Jesus Christ, both in our individual and corporate walk with Him. Jesus wants disciples, and He has the right to disciple us, if we are His, in every area of our life — our home, family, money, work, plans, hopes — and even our church! We are resolved to walk the path of radical discipleship with Jesus, believing that anything less is a denial of His Lordship. This means a readiness to change anything within our life, or within our church, that He points out to us.'

Unwillingness to change anything and everything that God would point out to us causes sections of many Christian Denominations to be frozen in space or, as Roy Pointer has pointed out, 'Many Sunday services are so alienated from contemporary Britain that church

attendance has become an adventure in time travel –
backwards. It is possible to join Medieval Anglicans,
Sixteenth Century Independents, Eighteenth Century
Methodists, Victorian Baptists and Salvationists and
Pre-War Pentecostals. Their language and liturgies
remain unchanged and they survive as cultural fossils in
Ecclesiastical strata'.[6]

His book is devoted to highlighting many Fellowships
within those Denominations that have adapted
effectively to change. The tragedy is that many others
are content to exist within a timewarp of thier own
making.

He who is the 'Ancient of Days' is still the God who
makes all things new.

The Challenge of Controversy
The productive promotion of truth is to be guarded.
Controversy and what the Bible calls, 'meaningless talk'
is to be guarded against. If the Christian is to have an
open mind to God then hobby-horses must be put out to
grass. Perhaps they should be shot.

The term hobby-horse, according to *Brewer's
Dictionary of Phrase and Fable*, refers to a light
wickerwork frame, appropriately draped, in which
someone gambolled in the old Morris dances. The name
is also applied to a child's toy, consisting of a stick
across which he straddles, with a horse's head at one
end. To 'ride a hobby-horse' was to play an infantile
game of which one soon tired. It now, of course, implies
the dwelling to excess on a pet theory: the transition to a
figure of speech is shown in one of Wesley's sermons:
'Everyone has, to use the cant term of the day, his
hobby-horse.'

The phrase Paul uses refers to a person who,
'promotes controveries rather than God's work'.[7]

Most of us can never imagine the analogy applying to ourselves. Hobby-horses are always mounts that other people ride. If one man's meat is another man's poison, then one man's hobby-horse is another man's Derby winner. Three things identify the rider.

1. *Lacking in Love*

The problem with people who ride hobby-horses is that they want all the road to themselves. The animal is fed fat on the rich fodder of prejudice, aptly described by Ambrose Bierce as, 'a vagrant opinion without any visible means of support.' Because of this all too often the cause is lost sight of and the issue becomes the fight itself. Spiritually, even if the cause is 'right', the cause is lost. When the Early Church argued about the necessity, or otherwise, of circumcision Paul wrote to the Galatians and said, 'For in Christ Jesus neither circumcision nor uncircumcision has any value. *The only thing that counts* is faith expressing itself through love.'[8]

What Paul said about circumcision could be said about one hundred and one other issues that become unnecessary battlefields in the Kingdom of God today. To major on minors is like being in the restaurant of the Titanic and arguing about how the steak should be cooked: unaware that as the food is going down so is the ship. As Christ is in the vessel, the Church is in no danger of going under but that, so often, is in spite of his disciples not because of them.

Very few, trapped in the white-hot inferno of the Bradford City football ground a few years ago would have been discussing the intricacies of the offside rule. Given the state of the world in general, and the ineffectiveness of so many sections of the church to reach their community in particular, one wonders how many 'big deals' there are left in the Kingdom of God that are worth fighting over.

2. *Lacking in Direction*

Referring to the 'goal of love' Paul remarks, 'Some have wandered away and turned to meaningless talk.' The hobby-horse rider does not set out to be unloving just as, in the same way, a traveller does not set out to get lost. The sad fact is that if a person is not prepared to look beyond the horse's ears, wandering is unavoidable and getting lost is to be expected. The road of Church history is littered with the grey corpses of beasts that have become stranded and rendered immobile in some marshy 'bypath meadow'; theological and procedural animals that had started out with the potential of thoroughbreds but turned out to be nothing more than hobby-horses. Left for dead in their ditch of bigotry, they serve only as grim reminders to the rest of us who pass by. Perhaps side-sliding is almost as bad as back-sliding.

3. *Lacking in Understanding*

One translation of the phrase 'meaningless talk' has, 'They have gone astray into a wilderness of words.' For the hobby-horse rider, words, trends and spiritual philosophies can become an end in themselves. Not only can the concept be allowed to take precedence over love but also over people, and sometimes over God Himself. The problem lies in the fact that hobby-horses tend to pull band wagons and band wagons tend to carry ideas. It matters not from which side of the Atlantic they come and whether or not they are housed in magazine, cassette or video tape.

What is important is that the order of, God – People – Concept, is not violated. To reverse the order is like finding a box and then buying a present to fit in it. Eventually both God and people will refuse to fit into something which is man made and contrived.

Certainly the hobby-horse rider is a danger to the Church; but he is also a danger to himself. For if he remains in the saddle too long, rider and horse merge into one. To reject his horse is to reject him. Objectively he has died.

In Acts 10 God had to speak to Peter in a vision three times before he would be willing to dismount his strongly held views and begin to listen to the new thing that God was saying. Even though, later on, he did try to climb back in the saddle and Paul had to 'withstand him to the face', his victory was a major testimony to Hobby Horse riders of every age.

When we can get to the place where we can comfortably dismount old prejudices without jumping on every new nag that passes the door we might be progressing some small way on the road to spiritual maturity with a mind that is open to God.

7: Open Hands

God is a generous God. He delights in giving. He always has. He gave Adam Eden and blessed him with Eve and, if that was not enough, added the world as a wedding present.

Even in its fallen state Creation takes our breath away. God made it in a riot of colour when He could have so easily have designed it in two shades of grey. No one forced Him to provide flowers or forests, starlight and sunsets: He just did.

We have taken a long look at many aspects of Openness. Much of it implies the giving of ourselves, the surrendering of our faculties, the offering of our lives in totality. Yet however much we give; it is impossible to outgive God. When Peter took it upon himself to remind the Lord about what a great sacrifice he, and the rest of the disciples, had made in following Him Jesus came back with the answer, 'I tell you the truth, no one who has left home or wife or brothers or parents or children for the sake of the kingdom of God will fail to receive many times as much in this age and, in the age to come, eternal life.'[1] Matthew's account adds houses and field and puts the interest at 'a hundred times as much'. Given that 'twice as much' would equate to one hundred per cent, 'a hundred times as much' is certainly some investment. With the collateral of heaven behind it and God as guarantor, few folk would argue with such rates of return. Why then is there such a reluctance on behalf of the people of God to receive that which God has provided for them? God's providence is our inheritance. All too often God has to say to His Church what Joshua said to Israel nearly three thousand five hundred years ago, 'How long will you wait before you begin to take possession of the land that the Lord, the God of your fathers, has given you?'[2]

What is often termed 'Prosperity Teaching' receives a bad press in many sections of the Christian Community. Sometimes the criticism is deserved. Taken to unscriptural extremes it degenerates into what can only be described as, The Theology of the Spoilt Child, the basic tenet of which is, 'I want it so I'll have it, now.'

In fairness, very few who teach on these lines take the subject to such unbiblical limits. In many instances they have brought to the Church a lost message, a timely word which comes against the 'spirit of poverty' embraced by so many sections of the Christian church. They have questioned the concept that, 'Living by Faith' is synonymous with, 'Living from hand to mouth'.

Neither should 'prosperity' be understood only in terms of that which is material and tangible. When one thinks of the prayer that the Apostle Paul prayed for the church at Ephesus one wonders if there is a prosperity teacher on earth that could match it. He says, 'I pray that out of His glorious riches He may strengthen you with power through His spirit in your inner being . . . that you may be filled to the measure of all the fullness of God.'[3] That's full!

What a tragedy when man, who was created for so much, settles for so little.

God can only give to people with open hands: hands that can reach to the other side of prayer – the place of receiving. There are five steps into God's reception area.

1. *I must accept that God wants to bless me*

Not everyone does. When we first come to Christ it is necessary to recognise that our good works cannot save us. Some struggle for years before they can come to terms with the fact that eternal life is a gift and cannot be earned or deserved. Eventually, we come to the place where we realise that salvation depends, not upon what we can do, but upon what Christ has done.

Having been brought into the Kingdom of God there is a tendency to continue to fight the same battle again when we are challenged to receive the promises that God has given His children. We complain that we are not deserving or important enough to be worthy of such lavish attention. It usually comes down to the fact that we do not feel 'loved enough'.

When we look at the encounter that Moses had with God at the Burning Bush, more than one of us will see a reflection of our own attitude to service. God wanted to put in his hands the responsibility of leading two million people into freedom but his fist was clenched tight in nervousness. He did not feel free to accept the charge.

The dialogue that Moses had with God sheds light on to a common dilemma. The reluctant hero argues that he cannot possibly be God's choice as he has never been eloquent and was currently slow of speech. It is remarkable that, those of us who profess to be so weak, always seem strong enough and quick enough, to tell the Lord that we know the will of God better than He does. When Moses struggled with God and told him that he could not obey because of who he was and what he was, God took up the challenge and used the same duelling instrument – He reminded Moses of His Name and of His status. 'I am the God of Abraham, Isaac and Jacob . . . I am who I am.' God never wanted his ability in the first place. He wanted his availability.

When Elijah was on Mount Carmel God took a sacrifice that was soaked in water and set fire to it. Here, God sets fire to a bush and it is Moses that goes away burning. He had approached the place far from tinder dry; saturated as he was by a poor self image, frustration and lack of fulfilment. He went away burning to prove for all time that God can set anyone ablaze.

2. *I must expect that God wants to bless me*
God told Joshua, 'I will give you every place that you set your foot.'[5] The places to which God was referring were not uninhabitated areas. The enemy lived there. It was occupied territory. Joshua was soon to learn that few of the places of blessing in Canaan were provided with Vacant Possession. This was important for the new commander to learn. When the people marched round Jericho it was not with an ambling and uncertain gait, accompanied by the scratching of heads and mutterings of, 'How on earth will we get in here?' The people were marking out *their* territory and claiming it. Every step was made with a firmer assurance until such faith had risen that it almost did not need a miracle for the walls to come down: subsidence alone would have done the job. The walls fell 'inwards' as an evidence that it really was an act of God that brought the victory about.

Joshua soon learned that the best blessings of God do not fall, like ripe cherries, on the heads of every Believer. They had to be claimed. They had to be fought for.

When they had come to the Jordan and needed to cross, it was not a matter of God opening the way and then them stepping out. Their leaders were told to stand in the water, silly though that might look to some, and then God would do His necessary part. They were not called to walk on the water but to walk into it. This act

143

displayed to God that they expected Him to act on their behalf. It was the action of the open hand.

Nor did God want these principles of faith to be locked away in some fousty Old Testament dispensationalism. Spiritual Warfare was a subject to be studied at every spritual Sandhurst, in every age and in every culture.

When the lepers came to Jesus he told them to go and show themselves to the priests – as evidence of their healing. As they looked down upon their rotting flesh they would have seen no significant change. The narrative says, 'As they went, they were cleansed.'[6] Once again, stepping out was the answer. By doing so they were declaring that they took Jesus at His word. They were articulating by their actions something that the writer to the Hebrews would one day put into words: that, 'Faith is being sure of what we hope for and certain of what we do not see.'[7]

Put another way, they were making provision for faith's fulfilment. As a young couple expecting their first child decorate a room as a nursery and purchase a push-chair before their child is born so, people with the open hand of faith, make preparation in advance for what they believe the Lord has promised to accomplish.

When there was a drought in the land Elisha received a word from the Lord. The message to the rulers of the nation was this, 'Make the valleys full of ditches.'[8] This was a prerequisite. If they believed that God was going to send the rain they were being asked to act accordingly. In response to their obedience the rain came and every ditch they dug was filled.

One wonders what God thinks of churches whose buildings are already full with people and who are praying for revival, but have no extension programme planned or preparations for a move to new premises.

How seriously does God take our praying for growth when the local minister is already fully stretched in his care for the flock and there is no provision for additional pastoral staff, the recognition and training of Elders, care groups or house groups for new converts.

The smallest child knows that when a cup is full, any sensible person stops pouring – the structure has reached its optimum capacity. Surely God is of no less intelligence. If buildings or ministries are filled to the limit, God too must stop pouring. Any fisherman knows that if his nets are filled to the point they are broken, all his fish may be lost.

Those of us who pray for another Day of Pentecost in which three thousand souls were added to the Church in one day, must stop and ask ourselves what would happen if God were to answer the prayer. When it comes to caring, counselling and discipling many churches could not cope with thirty, let alone three thousand.

One day a young pastor, struggling in his church and seeing so few people come to Christ, called on C H Spurgeon for advice. 'But surely you do not expect people to be converted every time you preach the Gospel', said Spurgeon. 'Oh no, of course not', replied the young man defensively. 'And that,' said the prince of preachers, 'is precisely the reason you fail to achieve your result.'

As the home prayer group interceded for Peter in his imprisonment they were disturbed by a knock on the door. The Scriptures record that when the servant girl Rhoda was sent to discover the reason for this intrusion in their great spiritual quest, she, recognising Peter ran back to the group, 'without opening the door'. When she related who was there she, possibly a new and impressionable convert, was told by the other members of the prayer cell group that she must be mad. Peter could not possibly be there because they were 'praying' for his release! As they were knocking on God's door with their request: God was knocking on their door with the answer. Open hands release the latch. Praying is of no use unless it is linked to hands that can receive. God measures our prayers by one yardstick: the preparation we are making for the fulfilment of our faith.

3. *I must ask to the limit of my faith*

There is something exciting about the story of the widow and her cruise of oil; but there is also something sad. Elisha had said to her, 'Go around all your neighbours for empty jars. Don't ask for just a few. Then go inside and shut the door behind you and your sons. Pour oil into all the jars and as each one is filled put it to one side.'[9]

The widow did this and the miracle started. The sad part comes next, 'When all the jars were full she said to her son, "Bring me another one", but he replied, "There is not a jar left." *Then* the oil stopped flowing.'

When the woman went out on her errand to her neighbours there was a point when she stopped and said to herself, 'I think I've got enough'. She had been told that when she came to that point in her expectancy, she was to come inside the house and 'close the door behind her'. There was a finality in the statement. It was a punctuation mark, a stop, at the end of her faith. It indicated when her expectancy had reached its fullest potential. There was no going out for more jars after this point. It is significant that in the middle of the miracle she was ready for more jars – its easier to believe in the middle of a miracle than it is when faced with 'empty vessels'. It was the same challenge that was presented to the ditch-diggers, the Jericho-joggers, the

Priests who crossed the Jordan, the ten lepers and now the widow. Yet again, the faith that is rewarded is the faith that makes provision.

In 2 Kings 13 we find a king in turmoil. Elisha was on his deathbed and Jehoash was worried about what was going to become of the kingdom should the prophet die.

Elisha told him to get a bow and some arrows and to imagine that outside the window were the enemies of Israel, the armies of Aram. As Jehoash pulled back the bow string the prophet put his hand on the king's hand and told him to fire the arrow from the east window. As he did so Elisha cried out, 'The Lord's arrow of victory, the arrow of victory over Aram!'

Elisha was introducing Jehoash to a vital lesson in faith: it is impossible to believe for something that you cannot imagine.

I was once approached by a lady, at the close of a meeting at which I had been the speaker, who told me that she had been praying for years for the salvation of her husband but without success. I asked her if she could imagine her husband ever becoming a Christian. She sullenly replied, 'Not really.' We talked for a while and I endeavoured to explain that God uses our imagination as a basis on which to build our faith. The next time I met her I discovered that she had bought a Bible for him in preparation for his conversion. The answer was on the way!

There are those who misunderstand this approach to prayer and delegate it in their thinking to no more than 'mind over matter'. It should be made clear that the tool of the imagination plays no part whatsoever in the miracle itself: it simply prepares the ground in which the seed of faith is to be sown. Jesus explained this when He said, 'Therefore I tell you, whatever you ask for in prayer, believe that you have received it, and it will be yours.'[10]

Jehoash was doing well to the point that the prophet was holding his hand. Unfortunately, when asked to walk in his own faith, like Peter, he began to sink.

Elisha now requested him to pick up the bundle of arrows that were left and strike them on the floor, imagining that he was beating the armies of Aram into the ground. He gathered the arrows together and gave the ground a hefty blow, the second was weaker and at the third he stopped. Elisha may have been on the point of death but this action, or inaction, of the king caused his spiritual adrenalin to pump and angrily he cries out, 'You should have struck the ground five or six times; then you would have defeated Aram and completely destroyed it. But now you will defeat it only three times.'

If only Israel had dug more ditches. If only the widow had gathered more jars. If only Jehoash had struck the ground more forcefully.

When Jesus was confronted by the blind man He asked him what may have seemed to some onlookers as an almost superfluous question, 'What would you that I should do unto you?' The man could have asked for a contribution to his begging bowl. He chose to 'go for gold' and ask for the biggest thing he could believe for, 'Lord Jesus, that I might receive my sight.' He got it.

When Peter and John were at the Beautiful Gate, a tourist attraction that drew crowds and beggars alike, a crippled man called out for some coins. Peter said, 'Silver or gold I do not have, but what I have I give you. In the name of Jesus Christ of Nazareth, walk.' What a miracle! He asked for alms, and got legs! Which goes to show that our generous God sometimes gives to open hands, 'Immeasurably more than all we ask or imagine'.[11]

Praise can often be the catalyst that causes our faith

to believe for God's best. 'Magnifying the Lord' is as strange a term as it is Scriptural. How can we make God any bigger? The answer is, of course, we can't. The use of a magnifying lens never makes the object any larger than it is. It just makes it larger to us. So in our worship, the inifinite God changes neither in shape nor in volume as we praise. What does take place is that we begin to appreciate what a powerful God He is. Our problems are seen in their true perspective and we can believe God for bigger things and greater victories.

How much can we honestly expect of God? Paul gives us the answer in his letter to the Romans, 'He who did not spare His own Son, but gave Him up for us all – how shall He not also, along with him, graciously give us all things.'[12]

4. *I must have hands that can relinquish as well as retain*
The story of Achan is a challenge. God had expressly commanded that when Jericho was taken no soldier was to take any of the spoils for himself. Achan, thinking he would never be discovered, took silver, gold and a Babylonian robe. The result of his disobedience stretched far beyond the floor of the tent in which they were hidden. The seventh chapter of the book of Joshua makes it clear that the transgression of this one man affected the whole of the people of God. His sin could be summed up in this: he had 'picked up' something from the enemies of God.

God told his people that he would not be with them anymore until they 'destroyed' whatever among them had been devoted to destruction'. It was a reminder of the words in Deuternonomy, 'The images of their gods you are to burn in the fire. Do not covet the silver and gold on them, and do not take it for yourselves, or you will be ensnared by it, for it is detestable to the Lord your God. Do not bring a detestable thing into your house or you, like it, will be set apart for destruction.'[13]

In other words, God could not deliver the enemy into their hands because their hands were already full of things that should not be there. The Psalmist speaking of the one with clean hands and a pure heart said, '*He will receive* blessing from the Lord and vindication from God his Saviour.'[14]

The twentieth century Christian may well worship at weekends in Zion but they are most likely to be working in modern-day Jerichos through the week. It can be all too easy to 'pick things up' – wrong attitudes, world-views, life-styles and a thousand and one other manifestations of the Babylonian robe.

The New Testament Christian has 'renounced secret and shameful ways' – they have dropped them. They have 'put off', the old ways, as one might discard old clothing, and 'put on' the new.[15]

The Communion table is a place where the Believer is called upon to take stock. 'Let a man examine himself and so let him eat of the bread.' Washing our hands before we eat was never a bad idea.

5. *My hands must be willing to give as well as receive*

God has not called us to be cul-de-sacs. He has commissioned us to be thoroughfares. He has called us to be 'stewards of His grace', not 'hoarders of His blessing.'

When the Christian acts in obedience to this principle the miracle of the loaves and fishes is re-enacted and the giver is left with more than he started with. Bible writers separated by centuries, culture and geographical distance all bear testimony to the same phenomenon.

In Proverbs we read, 'One man gives freely, yet gains even more; another withholds unduly, but comes to poverty. A generous man will prosper; he who refreshes others will himself be refreshed.'

Malachi says, 'Bring the whole tithe into the storehouse, that there may be food in my house. Test me in this, says the Lord Almighty, and see if I will not throw open the floodgates of heaven and pour out so much blessing that you will not have room enough for it.'

Luke records the words of Jesus, 'Give and it will be given to you. A good measure, pressed down, shaken together and running over will be poured into your lap. For with the measure you use, it will be measured to you.'[16]

These verses have been misused by some in the past but that does not detract from the truth of them. 'Reaping what you sow' may be a threat to the guilty but it is a precious promise to the righteous.

What is true financially is also true emotionally. Those who are warm towards others are the most likely to find their friendliness reflected.

Epilogue

Psalm 24 has been quoted more than once during the course of this book. This is because reading it again recently I felt that it had much to say on the whole subject of the Open Life.

The picture is of Christ returning, victorious from battle, with the spoils of war in His possession. As he approaches the city the Holy Spirit calls out for the Gatekeeper to open the doors and allow Him entrance. Three times the Gatekeeper substitutes argument for obedience and at the close of the chapter the doors remain locked.

God calls upon His Church to grant Him unhindered access. In some cases Ancient Doors, long locked, offer stubborn resistance. The hinges have rusted with the passing of time.

At the point that the Gatekeeper of the Soul surrenders his will, penetrating oil begins to flow, the doors open. The King has come home.

'Here I am! I stand at the door and knock. If anyone hears my voice and opens the door, I will come in and eat with him, and he with me' (Revelation 3:20).

Notes

Chapter One

1. Luke 7:39
2. John 2:25
3. Kings 14:1–20
4. 2 Samuel 14:14
5. Psalm 62:8
6. Hebrews 4:12
7. Matthew 23
8. Acts 5:4
9. *Destined for the Throne*
10. 1 Samuel 10
11. Philippians 4:13
12. Revelation 3:1
13. *Restoring your Spiritual Passion*

Chapter Two

1. Jeremiah 2:1. The margin of the NIV indicates that the Masoretic text has 'my glory'.
2. Romans 1:23
3. Exodus 33:19
4. Romans 1:20
5. John 1:14, Hebrews 1:3, 2 Corinthians 4:6
6. Colossians 1:16
7. John 2:11
8. John 17:22
9. Ephesians 3:21
10. Isaiah 60:1–3
11. Psalm 50:2
12. 2 Corinthians 3:18

Chapter Three

1. Revelation 2:7, 11, 17, 29; 3:6, 13, 22
2. Acts 7:2, 51–53, 57
3. 1 Samuel 3:1
4. 1 Samuel 2:29
5. Psalm 66:18
6. Proverbs 28;9, Isaiah 1:15, John 9:31
7. James 5:16
8. Acts 24:24, 25
9. Psalm 126:5, 6
10. 2 Timothy 4:3, 4
11. John 6:66, Matthew 13:13
12. Hebrews 13:17
13. Hosea 10:12
14. Job 23:16
15. Psalm 119:67, 71
16. 2 Samuel 14:14

Chapter Four

1. 2 Corinthians 4:4
2. 1 Peter 2:9
3. Genesis 11:31, 32
4. Genesis 12:7
5. Genesis 26
6. Hebrews 3:19–4:2
7. Hebrews 11:27
8. Isaiah 22:1
9. 2 Corinthians 4:17, 18
10. Genesis 13:14
11. 3 John 9, 10
12. Psalm 68:6
13. Proverbs 17:24

14. John 4:35
15. James 2:14–18
16. Ecclesiastes 7:10
17. Luke 19:13 (KJV)
18. John 19:31
19. Hebrews 12:2
20. Mark 15:15
21. Matthew 6:22, 23
22. Philippians 3:13, 14
23. Proverbs 29:18 (KJV)
24. Daniel 11:32 (KJV)
25. 2 Timothy 1:12
26. 2 Corinthians 2:11
27. Philippians 4:19
28. Obadiah 17
29. Jeremiah 9:23, 24
30. Psalm 119:105
31. Revelation 3:17
32. 2 Kings 5:11, 12
33. Oswald Chambers, *Conformed in His Image*

Chapter Five

1. Proverbs 4:23
2. Jeremiah 17:9, Genesis 6:5, Matthew 15:18, 19
3. Psalm 26:2, 139:23, 24
4. Psalm 44:21
5. 1 Samuel 16:7
6. Hebrews 4:12, 13
7. Psalm 24:3, 4
8. Ezekiel 14:1–15
9. 1 Corinthians 3:13
10. 2 Corinthians 5:11, 14, 18–20; 6:2
11. Acts 16:14, 15
12. John 8:28
13. Richard Foster, *Celebration of Discipline*

14. Hebrews 5:8, 9; 2:10, 18
15. Isaiah 6:8
16. Ephesians 6:6
17. Revelation 1:7, 18
18. Jeremiah 19:9
19. 1 Peter 3
20. Joseph Aldrich, *Life Style Evangelism* (page 36)
21. Isaiah 62:12
22. Exodus 8:16–19
23. Exodus 28:29, 30
24. 2 Corinthians 6:11, 7:3, Philippians 1:7
25. 1 John 4:19–21
26. Romans 12:10; 15:5,7, Galatians 5:13; 6:2, Colossians 3:13 1 Thessalonians 5:11, 1 Peter 4:9, Hebrews 10:24, James 5:16, 1 John 4:17
27. John 15:15
28. Psalm 68:6
29. Michael Griffiths, *Cinderella with Amnesia*
30. Matthew 23:37
31. 1 Timothy 3:15
32. Psalm 51:10, 17
33. Psalm 34:18
34. William Barclay, *New Testament Words* (page 240)
35. Mark 6:52
36. Job 23:16 (KJV)
37. Ezekiel 11:19, 2 Corinthians 5:17
38. Ephesians 3:17
39. Colossians 1:20
40. Isaiah 53:5
41. Psalm 29:11, John 14:27
42. Romans 8:6, Isaiah 48:6

43. Luke 7:50; 8:24, 48

Chapter Six

1. Romans 12:2
2. 1 Corinthians 2:16
3. 2 Corinthians 10:5
4. Philippians 4:8
5. Luke 16:8
6. Roy Pointer, *Why Churches Grow*
7. 1 Timothy 1:4
8. Galatians 5:6

Chapter Seven

1. Luke 18:29, 30, Matthew 19:29

2. Joshua 18:3
3. Ephesians 3:14−19
4. Exodus 3 and 4
5. Joshua 1:3
6. Luke 17:14
7. Hebrews 11:1
8. 2 Kings 3:16
9. 2 Kings 4:3, 4
10. Mark 11:24
11. Ephesians 3:20, Acts 3:6
12. Romans 8:32
13. Deuteronomy 7:25, 26
14. Psalm 24:5
15. 2 Corinthians 4:2, Romans 13:12−14
16. Proverbs 11:24, Malachi 3:10, Luke 6:38

Other Marshall Pickering Paperbacks

RICH IN FAITH

Colin Whittaker

Colin Whittaker's persuasive new book is written for ordinary people all of whom have access to faith, a source of pure gold even when miracles and healing seem to happen to other people only.

The author identifies ten specific ways to keep going on the road to faith-riches, starting where faith must always begin—with God himself, the Holy Spirit, the Bible, signs and wonders, evangelism, tongues and finally to eternal life with Christ.

OUR GOD IS GOOD

Yonggi Cho

This new book from Pastor Cho describes the blessings, spiritual and material, that reward the believer. Yonggi Cho presents his understanding of the fullness of salvation, bringing wholeness to God's people.

HEARTS AFLAME
Stories from the Church of Chile

Barbara Bazley

Hearts Aflame is a book suffused with love for the large, sometimes violent country of Chile and joy at the power of the Gospel taking root.

Each chapter is a story in itself, telling of some encounter, episode of friendship that has left its mark on the author's life.

THE PLIGHT OF MAN AND THE POWER OF GOD

Dr Martin Lloyd-Jones

The text of one of the highly esteemed sermons given by Dr Martin Lloyd-Jones, based on verses from Romans, Chapter One, focuses on our need to be entirely committed to the Christian gospel.

Dr Lloyd-Jones highlights the uniqueness of the faith. Because of this he stresses the necessity of our absolute commitment to Christ and his call to us.

This book will be of great interest to all thoughtful Christians and of help to preachers, speakers and students.

THE NATURAL TOUCH

Kim Swithinbank

Some people think of 'evangelism' as knocking on doors, reading your Bible on the train or starting up conversations with strangers in which you get on to the four-point-plan-of salvation as quickly as possible. Some of these activities we would do, others we'd cringe at doing.

In his first book, Kim Swithinbank says that sharing our hope in Christ is something that we are *all* asked to do. It should be as natural as breathing to us.

Taking us through the most common obstacles which keep people away from Christianity, he shows how we can develop a lifestyle which is attractive and compelling for Christ.

Kim Swithinbank is Director of Evangelism at All Souls, Langham Place.

If you wish to receive *regular information* about *new books*, please send your name and address to:

London Bible Warehouse
PO Box 123
Basingstoke
Hants RG23 7NL

Name..

Address ....

....

....

....

I am especially interested in:
- ☐ Biographies
- ☐ Fiction
- ☐ Christian living
- ☐ Issue related books
- ☐ Academic books
- ☐ Bible study aids
- ☐ Children's books
- ☐ Music
- ☐ Other subjects